Also by BRETT RUTHERFORD

POETRY
Songs of the I and Thou (1968)
City Limits (1970)
The Pumpkined Heart: Pennsylvania Poems (1973, 2017)
Thunderpuss: In Memoriam (1987)
Prometheus on Fifth Avenue (1987)
At Lovecraft's Grave (1988)
In Chill November (1990)
Poems from Providence (1991, 2011)
Twilight of the Dictators (with Pieter Vanderbeck) (1992, 2009)
Knecht Ruprecht, or the Bad Boy's Christmas (1992)
The Gods As They Are, On Their Planets (2005, 2012, 2017)
Things Seen in Graveyards (2007, 2017)
Doctor Jones and Other Terrors (2008)
Anniversarius: The Book of Autumn (1984, 1986, 1996, 2011)
Trilobite Love Song (2014)

PLAYS
Night Gaunts: An Entertainment Based on the Life and Work of H.P. Lovecraft (1993, 2005)

NOVELS
Piper (with John Robertson) (1985, 2017)
The Lost Children (1988, 2017)

AS EDITOR/PUBLISHER
May Eve: A Festival of Supernatural Poems (1975)
Last Flowers: The Romance Poems of Edgar Allan Poe and Sarah Helen Whitman (1987, 2003, 2008, 2011).
M.G. Lewis's *Tales of Wonder*. Annotated edition (2010, 2012).
A.T. Fitzroy. *Despised and Rejected*. Annotated edition (2010).
Death and the Downs: The Poetry of Charles Hamilton Sorley. Annotated edition (2010).
Tales of Terror: The Supernatural Poem Since 1800, 2 volumes (2015, 2016)

AN EXPECTATION OF PRESENCES

NEW POEMS & REVISIONS

BRETT RUTHERFORD

THE POET'S PRESS
PITTSBURGH, PA

Copyright © 2012 by Brett Rutherford
All Rights Reserved
ISBN 0-922558-69-8
The author places this work in the Public Domain
on January 1, 2030.

Some of the poems in this book have appeared
in the following publications:
Sensations Magazine, East Side Monthly (Providence),
Literature and Gender (Longman), and
The Rhode Island Writers Circle Anthology (2008, 2010)
Rev 1.2

This is the 202nd publication of
THE POET'S PRESS
2209 Murray Avenue #3/ Pittsburgh, PA 15217
www.poetspress.org

TABLE OF CONTENTS

OUT HOME
   Imaginary Playmate   11
   Child Sex Criminal   15
   Doctor Jones   19
   Torrance   26
   Nights at the Strand   39
   Monday Miss Schreckengost Reads Us
      Little Black Sambo   44
   Out Home   51
   The Pines   57
   Brown Derby   61
   Sinkholes   62
   The Butcher Knife   66
   What's It to Me   67
   All I Know About My Father   69
   English Breakfasts   71
   The Blue Boy   73
   At the Funeral Home   76
   To My Stepfather   79
   Mr. Penney's Books   81

LOVE SPELLS
   When Did I Know   87
   Irises   91
   The Obsession   93
   A Year and a Day   100
   What She Was Like   102
   Uranium Boy   107
   Hyllus and the Charioteer   109
   Burnt Offering   110
   Hephaistion and Alexander   112
   Triptych   114
   28-20-18/ 50-22-19   119
   The Loft on Fourteenth Street   123
   Steven, Twenty Years After   129
   Dan's T-Shirt   134
   The Price   136
   El Precio   137
   Love Spells   138
   See You   140

PAST THE MILLENNIUM
    Sneakers   145
    Old Poet Glimpsed on the Subway   147
    The 20th Century   148
    Solzhenitsyn in New York   150
    The Linden Tree in Prague   153
    Sarajevo Dollhouse   159
    August Recess   163
    October Thoughts in Wartime   164
    Presidential Update   166
    Theology 101   167
    The Black Huntsman   168
    Veterans' Day Parade   171
    The Prophet Bird   173

ARS POETICA
    With Poe on Morton Street Pier   179
    The Garden of Numa Pompilius   182
    Epigrams   185
    Danny and Beatrice   186
    Arabesques on Early Modern Mathematics   191
    Pepper and Salt   195
    Spool   198
    On A Chinese Fan   200
    Labyrinth   202
    The Periodic Table: Hydrogen   204
    eve is a palindrome   206
    Ice Storm   208
    Lucy, A Verse Mystery   209
    Chance Cards in the *Wuthering Heights* Board Game   219
    Something There Is in the Attic   220
    The Vanished Chapel   223

HUMORESQUES
    A Night in Eddie's Apartment   227
    The Adventures of Sock-Puppet Peter   231
    HPL At the Newsstand   240
    Ballet of the Hors d'Oeuvre   243
    The New Tenant   246
    Two Philosophy Students   249
    Autumn on Mars   251

TWO VERSE PLAYS
    Carlota, Empress of Mexico   255
    The Prisoner   272

SYMPHONIE FANTASTIQUE
    Symphonie Fantastique   281
    Keziah Mason   285
    Keziah's Geometry Lessons   288
    True Friends   292
    Autumn on Pluto   294
    Dawn   297
    The Eye, The Mind, The Tentacle   305
    Hearing the Wendigo   309
    Squanto's Wind   311
    Here At the Point   315
    The Collectors   319
    Quand Il Pleut, Il Pleut des Financiers   321
    Not A Hymn to Venus   324
    Portrait of Dorian Gray   326
    Miners' Cemetery, Atacama, Chile   331
    Night Shift   334
    The Secret Tree   337
    Since the Old Ones Came Back to Earth   339
    An Expectation of Presences   342
    Bai Hu, The White Tiger   345

ABOUT THE POEMS   351

ABOUT THE POET   362

ABOUT THIS BOOK   363

OUT HOME

IMAGINARY PLAYMATE

It was my secret place
away from bath-time and spanking,
Grandfather's grizzled hugs,
the cries of the baby brother,
away from heat and brambles,
blackberry barb and poison ivy,
a cool-air haven
where the acrid fumes
of coke oven smoke
never intruded:
the "spring-house,"
a covered well, actually,
a cobwebbed shed
of cool-sweated pump and pipe.
Here I could sit
behind its plank door,
imagine another door,
flat on the concrete,
might open *downward*
to a treasure cave,
a city of runaways,
a subterranean launchpad
for moon rockets.

One day a man was there,
crouching inside
beneath a straw hat,
a shoulder pack,
more frightened of me,
it seemed, than I of him.

I sat beside him
on the cold stone lip
of the gurgling well.
His whispered words
were barely louder
than the distant coal trucks,
the chirring cicadas.

His name was Eric,
a young man, yet
bigger than my father.
He asked about my mother,
my teacher, my friends
I would see again
in second grade in the fall.
"Too bad your mother is married,"
he said. "She's pretty.
I watched her from the road."

Two weeks he hid there,
sleeping all morning.
I brought him cookies.
He taught me games.
Once, I touched
the soft blond beard
that glazed his cheekbones.
I could tell him anything.

Soap opera organ
rose to a frenzy
on the oval-windowed
new television
as some one yelled
"Kidnapped!
Our son has been kidnapped!"
What's *kidnap?* I ask my mother.
She, ironing, from the other room:
*That's when they steal a child
and then ask for money.*

I thought it might be fun
to be kidnapped.
I might even get to keep
some of the money.
Just watch out for strange cars,
my mother warned.

One day I mentioned Eric
at the dinner table.

"That's all he talks about,"
my mother explained.
"That's his friend,
his imaginary playmate."
My father grew angry.
They shouted
as I read comics in the attic.

One day, my father took me
to a roadside tavern.
He sat in the back
with his band leader,
played an illegal
slot machine.
A strange man came in,
saw me alone,
gave me a nickel
to buy potato chips.

As my father returned
I asked my new friend,
"Can I have another nickel?"
My father exploded,
shouted at the stranger,
"No one gives my kid money!"

Strangers seemed kinder to me
than parents.
I imagined kidnapped children,
sweets and sodas everywhere,
fresh bread from the oven,
mountains of comic books,

a long wait for the ransom,
maybe never.

At home, the spring-house was locked.
My mother doled out dinner:
government surplus beef
and slices of cheese
off a long square loaf.

Some nights we ate bread
and gravy and radishes.

I stayed indoors all summer.
Sometimes at night
I thought I saw someone
cross from the poplars,
to the spring-house, then back again,
a lanky form darting
from shadow to shadow.

I sleepwalked many nights,
awaking against the locked
front door. On other nights
I dreamt a new door
at the back of the closet.
I opened it, to another door,
and yet another, until sleep
vacuumed me to darkness.

I never mentioned Eric again.

Years later I heard
of the men who slept
in the nearby foothills,
setting up camp
in the abandoned ovens —
draft dodgers avoiding
the Korean War call-up.

Years after that I suddenly
remembered him again —
his soft tenor voice in the shadow,
the friend to whom I said,

"Would you kidnap me someday?
I'll never tell ... I promise."

CHILD SEX CRIMINAL

At six
I find the place,
the tender glans
whose finger-rub
in gentle circles
makes me tremble,
till sparklers go off
from brain-stem
to end of spine.
It was, and remained
    my secret,
an under-blanket ritual.

So much to mind
about the body's plumbing:
dry underwear,
    toilet concealment,
as though the outcome
of last night's dinner
was a national secret.

Nervous Aunt Thelma
    chides us:
How can you have a bathroom
next to the kitchen?
The sound of flushing
    sickens me.

First grade
    you raised your hand
    and asked to go
    to the cave-cool bathroom

Second grade boys
    march to the bathroom
expected to pee
    on the teacher's schedule.

I confide to the principal
at the next urinal:
I don't have to go —
I'm just pretending.

On homeward bus,
half-dozen boys
hunch over, wince
from the agony
of holding it in
just five more minutes.
One day I could not hold it,
walked stained
    and dripping
to shouts and a spanking.

In second grade
my penis rebels
against conformity,
an unzipped peeper
as Miss McReady
explains subtractions.

I touch the spot.
It springs to attention.
Suzie, who gave me
the chicken pox, stares
from the cross-aisle seat
and giggles. *Five*
minus three is two.

A nature book
nests on a restricted shelf —
NOT TO BE REMOVED
FROM CLASSROOM —
tells all about spiders.
I take it home one night
to show my mother,
devour by moonlight
long after the lights-out,

then slide it back
to its shelf-place
at the start of school-day.

But someone saw,
and ran to tell Miss Macready.
Now books the other children
may borrow,
I am not allowed to borrow.
"We don't loan books
to thieves,"
my teacher tells me.

We learn to read music.
After I was out with measles,
I return to find them singing
with flats and sharps. I have
no idea what they are doing.
Miss McReady will not explain.
I am trapped forever
in the white bread, white key
C-Major scale.

My next report card
alerts my parents:
**DISOBEYS SCHOOL
REGULATIONS.**

My mother assumes
it's over the book
brought home by stealth
and just as quietly
restored.

Suzie and Miss Macready
whisper and glare at me.
I don't mind much:
I read what I want
and when I want to,
break rules
I find ridiculous.

I have already decided
there is no god.
I will never sing in a church choir.
I will not pee on demand.
I am marked for life:

thief,
rule-breaker,
child sex criminal.

DOCTOR JONES

1
He drives a black Ford V8 Cabriolet.
It has a gold top, gold wheel spokes,
huge, round, cracked headlamps
glowing like yellow, bloodshot eyes.
His name is Alphonse Perry Jones.
That's *Doctor* Jones to you, little fellow.
He went to the War in Nineteen-Eighteen,
right out of medical school,
sent to the front in France
    with a black bag and a kit.
The soldier boys were brought in by the dozens.
The routine was simple — a swig of whisky
    the only anesthetic —
roll up the sleeves or the trouser cuffs.
Two men to pin the soldier down —
he didn't mind the sawing.
He never vomited the way the aides did.
He didn't mind the screams. In fact
    he somewhat grew to enjoy them,
    phonemes of agony, no two alike.
His eyes that hadn't focused well
    on parting flesh and severed arteries
    now studied each push and pull,
almost a rhythm to the saw thrusts
    and the soldier's scream,
in and out almost
    like lovemaking.
Sometimes the tourniquet and
    cauterizing took.
Sometimes they bled to death
    blubbering, eyes rolled
    to egg whites.
The nurses turned away. He
put his hand against the carotid
to feel the last spasms.

It looked like a benediction
but it was a taking —
   there, there it is,
   you're dead now.

After months at the Front,
dodging the Germans
and the gassy, shifting lines,
he is the only doctor left.
No one will eat with him.
The men whisper and stare,
sleep turned away
   with their guns loaded.
He does not care.
   They obey his orders.
The great tide of wounded keeps coming,
never enough crutches or bandages.
A hecatomb of hands and feet,
arms to the elbow, legs to the knee
fester unburied in a nearby trench.
Too bad the Armistice came so soon.

But that was long ago, years past
   and a drawer of tarnished medals
to prove he had been there, done that.
Late afternoon he rides
   the hills and hollows,
follows the yellow buses,
   watches the scrawny boys
     with their cowboy lunch boxes
    as they run to their mothers.
There beside him, his little book
with the names and addresses,
there,
     the black bag
       with everything he needs.
His name is Alphonse Perry Jones.
That's *Doctor* Jones to you, little fellow.
And he does house calls.

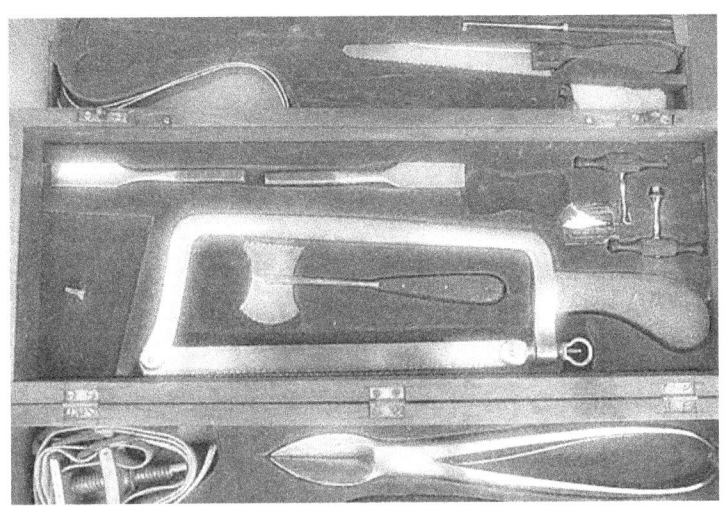

2
Five years ago I remembered you,
Doctor Jones. Five years ago
I tried to write this poem —
three times the pen
    touched down upon the empty page
three times
    my hands shook uncontrollably.

Are some things better not
remembered,
as flesh forgets wounds?
No, even flesh does not
forget: pale scars
are always there;
the ghosts of fractures
act up on rainy days.

We do not forget:
we crystallize around
our childhood terrors.

I see you, country doctor:
gaunt and cadaverous,
goateed and spectacled,
an old man towering
above my weakness.
Your fingers circle
my pencil-thin arms
as you chide my parents

Don't you feed this child?
He's all skin and bones.
Your cold hammer knocks
and my knees kick at you;
the stethoscope,
so cold I stop breathing.
You send me home
with cod liver pills,
which now supplement
the government surplus meat
and cheese we live on.

Soon Mother shows me
your sinister car.
That's Doctor Jones, she says.
If you don't do what you're told
he'll come some night
and have your leg off.

3
I go to school now
in a place called Hecla.
The school door faces
the grim machineries
of a coal mine.

From the back
of the school bus
I sometimes see
your black Ford
behind our dust cloud.

Sometimes a boy gets off,
runs down a lane,
down which your car
makes a slow turn,
following.
I never see
how it ends.

When I come home,
the endless rumble
of coal trucks
feeding the coke evens
drowns out
the comings and goings
of your car,
but I know you are there.

More than one night
I have spied those yellow headlights
with their tired veins glimmering,
slowing and stopping,
slowing and stopping
as though you watched
our windows for the dark-out.

I will not sleep
where a door is open,
see gaunt and bearded specters
in the musty closets.
The rats in the cellar,
the giant spiders
in the blackness of the attic,
the quicksand pools
out back behind
the slag-heaps
are minor terrors
beside you.

This year I watch locusts
sprout by the thousands
from tree and earth,
endure a hurricane
that rips the arms
from the Lombardy poplars,
see my first movie
where Nemo's ship
held fast by tentacles
breaks free of the giant squid
in a harpoon battle.

These things are as nothing
when my mother walks
to the telephone and says,
"All right, you little brat,
I'm calling Doctor Jones
right now!"

I hear myself still,
shrilly screaming,
bounding up steps,
closing my door,
waiting for the sound
of the gliding car.

Dark nights I sleepwalk
to escape you.

4
Five years ago I remembered you,
Doctor Jones. Five years ago
I tried to write this poem —
three times the pen
    touched down upon the empty page
three times
    my hands shook uncontrollably.

You are still everywhere:
    the doctor
    the dentist
    the barber, even, pressing me down
        in his innocent chair
you are still there
    in every unwanted touching.
You make every touch unwanted.

My mother is dead
and cannot erase you.
My father tells me you never existed,
that there was no doctor named Jones,
that no such name was ever spoken
    in his presence,
something your mother did to you,
some kind of mental abuse…

yet why do I know all three of your names,
the yellow-white bristles of your beard,
your medals and how you got them?
Why do I spy, within your plain black bag,
the reddish-brown leather
    of the American-made kit
    with its amputation bone saw,
    the finger saw,
    the metacarpal saw?

His name is Alphonse Perry Jones.
That's *Doctor* Jones to you, little fellow.
We'll have that leg off in no time.

TORRANCE

1
It had a name, and an associated dread.
Even small children knew of it:
   a place to be sent
     if you turned out crazy
        were deemed retarded
           touched yourself too often
     hurt someone   or killed your father
A place they emptied the jails into
   with that special class of men
   too evil to live with ordinary killers
A place where the deformed,
   the epileptic,
   the melancholic
were secreted away.

No one seemed ever
   to come back from Torrance.
Aunt Thelma went,
   a "nervous breakdown."
Her husband hastily
   remarried

    her cousin Irma
    (so alike they could have been sisters).
If you went once
    to the sunny wardroom
    to check in on a relative
you probably never went again —
something about the screams
    from the floor below,
the vacant stare of the patients
sunning themselves,
scalp scars and skull concavities,
mumbling   drooling
or the loquacious residents
eager to share the fact
that they were Jesus, Jahweh
or Marie Antoinette,
or the poignant plea
"What news from the Holy Land?
Have the Crusaders
    taken Jerusalem?"

White coat doctors
smoked in the corridors.
Strict nurses and burly attendants
kept everyone behaved.
You never quite understood
why suddenly they'd seize
a seemingly calm one

Now, now, you've done it again —
    Didn't I tell you? —
        It's off to your room now —
attendant waiting
    with that special jacket
        just at the edge of vision.

You never saw a syringe
but you knew,
if it were your lot
to come here,
endless needles would jab at you,

and you would wake screaming
in a padded place with but
   one window
and no one would hear you,
hear you
ever...

No, if you saw that once,
   you'd never be back to see
   Aunt Thelma,
your mouth dry
with the thought
They could keep me here,
   if only they knew—
      knew what I've done...

Built in 1919,
a red brick mansion
by any standard.
Handsome arches,
a dayroom lit
like a conservatory.
The director dined
on the finest linen and china,
the best food.
The doctors employed
the latest techniques.
Once you had signed away
the prisoner, the child,
   the broken-down wife,
they were free to experiment.
They opened skulls
   as smoothly
   as the director's wife
   scooped into a boiled egg,
poked around, sometimes removed
   a tumor or swelling.
If a criminal became
   a drooling idiot,
   what loss to society
if but one clue

to the brain's mysteries
were uncovered?

Then came the drugs,
and the Great Machine
that shock-erased bad memories,
    at least some of the time
        for some of the patients.
Too bad if they could no longer
remember their Shakespeare
or the best five years of their lives —
at least they were spared the knife.

Among the good doctors,
    a few were evil,
one, perhaps, as evil
as the jacketed murderers,

one, perhaps, who had been there
when the place opened
hard on the end
of the First World War.
He would have been a surgeon,
not qualified to touch
the seat of divinity the brain,
but there in reserve

when they hurt themselves
or one another, setting the bones,
stitching the flesh of would-be
    suicides.
Once in a great while
an amputation was needed,
and he was ready
with his red-lined surgeon's case

    amputation saw
    metacarpal saws trephines
        and knives.

Just like the War! he would
say wistfully,
downing a whiskey
and shining his instruments.
This bone saw, he'd tell
his colleagues,
dates back to 1878,
fine British workmanship.

He didn't much like
the modern anesthetics,
was heard to say
There is a music to pain.

Perhaps for some years
he was the Night Doctor,
the only one who saw
while the good staff
slept in their homes
what a madhouse really is
when the moon hits it:

how the attendants,
for certain favors,
undid the doors,
and certain patients,

(even the murderers)
got into rooms
and did what they wanted —
or what was wanted —
in the rooms of others,

how there were dances
and music,
and the attendants
laughed as they set
the mad against the feeble-minded,
the criminal against the paranoiac,
    for sport
    for power

and if anyone revealed
the *Danse Macabre*
and its participants,
who would believe them?

Patient exhibited
    paranoid delusions.
Patient presented
    self-inflicted wounds.

How many decades
did the mad minister the mad?
how many post-partum melancholic
wives were sent here and abandoned?
    how many incorrigible inverts
        lobotomized?
how many "nervous breakdowns"
broken with electric shock?
Only the nearby graveyard
with its tiny, numbered stones
could give a count.

And how did it pass
that the Night Doctor
came to be known
in all the surrounding

countryside
as "Doctor Jones?"
His black Ford Cabriolet
with its yellow round lamps
prowled the back roads.
Sometimes he followed
the school buses, marked
where all the small boys lived.
He had a list
and he made house calls.

Why did my mother say:

He drives out of Torrance,
and that's where he takes you.
To the crazy house.
And he puts you in a room.
And he ties you down.
And he opens the leather bag
and there's a box inside,
    a box lined in red

And that's where he gets them,
the knives and saws.
And he'll take your legs,
and then your arms,
and you'll see it all happen,
and you'll feel everything.

And they'll keep you there,
in a room,
no arms   no legs
   in a bed
   in a room with one tiny window
and anyone could come in
and do anything to you…

2
Torrance
   is in ruins,
     has been for decades.
You walk on glass
   and broken tiles,
the walls
   graffiti-covered
   reveal the thoughts
   of marauding teens —

ARE YOU SCARED YET?
   the first one asks

Y'ALL SHOULD BE!
   says the second.

In the ruined
   lower level,
bearable by day
in slant of sunbeam —

unthinkable on
   moonless nights —

a night-dank corridor
is lined with doors
doors into tiny rooms
whose bare bricks
might once
have been padded

a prison-slit window
at the top of each,
just large enough
to emit those screams
the thick trees muffled,
just large enough
to admit a bat
   or a spider.

What would have been
the day-room,
sunny once,
the red brick arches
and tall trees mocking
beyond the doors and windows

just as some corridors end now
in glimpses of field
   and twisted tree branch,
just as snarls of vine intrude
with the illusion
   that outside and inside
   might one day change places

or was the outside world
seen from door frame
through door frame
through outer arches
a white-eyed Moloch
whose leering face
threatened an outer world
a thousand times worse
than padded walls?

Did the attendants
and the Night Doctor
permit these vistas,
only to tell them
Go ahead and try.
Escape from Torrance,
and the whole countryside
will be on the lookout.
Search parties and guns,
rednecks and howling dogs
will track you down.

Those who left
and then came back
were never even half
of what they had been before,
their glazed eyes
    vacant
until the day
their numbered stone
was set in soil.

The words boys scrawl
on these derelict walls
do not convey their own
despair so much as what
oozes from the brickwork:

DON'T LET THEM BURN YOU!

ENTER THE BLACK HOLE!

I AM GOING TO DIE!

and perhaps the most
disturbing one,
because the truest:

FUCK MY DEAD BODY.

3
In my dreams
the brick edifice
still stands intact
in moonlight

three thousand souls
are packed inside —
none are sleeping —
six thousand eyes
and hands tensed
and waiting —

the black Ford Cabriolet
with its gold wheel spokes
and round-eyed headlamps
pulls up in front

and the gaunt specter
of the Night Doctor
lifts something in burlap —
something still moving? —
and hoists it
over his shoulder,

fumbling for keys,
he vanishes
into a stairwell,
his private entrance
to the lower rooms —

just another boy
who disobeyed his mother,
touched himself
   in the wrong place,
reminded his stepfather
too much of his father —

who will notice
one more scream
in the chorus of screams
from those cellar windows?

Anyone hearing
just shook his head
and shuddered,
joking nervously:

*Oh, that's Torrance,
the people in Torrance.
You can hear them
on summer nights.
The screaming is bad,
but the laughing,
that's worse. To be
in such a place and laugh —
now THAT'S crazy.*

4
There are no ghosts at Torrance,
not in the ruined corridors,
the pain cells, the solitary
padded rooms. Perhaps the mad
already lost their ghosts here,
their ectoplasm leaking out
through the drilled skull holes,
passing with the shock current,
up and out the chimneys.
The ghosts of murderers move on,
assuredly, to crime scenes,

or to the cradles of budding
psychopaths. They fled this place.
The doctors and attendants
died in their beds, had proper wakes,
widows and heirs at the graveside,
stones with their names and dates.

    No, what screams here is the ghost
of malice, and cruelty and power,
the soul of evil that says:

> *I am the Night Doctor.*
> *I can do anything to anyone,*
> *and I have found the place*
> *in which to do it.*
>
> *I'm glad we have these*
> *little evenings together,*
> *so glad we found*
> *our mutual interest.*
>
> *It's not easy for me*
> *to get you out.*
> *For chess, I tell them.*
> *I see you've laid*
> *the instruments in perfect order.*
> *You could have your own practice*
> *when they let you out of here.*
> *No, not for a while yet.*
>
> *Everything is ready.*
> *Would you like to see*
> *what I've got in this sack?*

NIGHTS AT THE STRAND

The Strand Theater, Scottdale, PA

As the lights dim and the tattered curtain
rustled and parted with a creak-crank
of unseen wheels and pulleys, as a boy's eyes
widen to a dark screen grown suddenly bright
and huge — not the tiny ovoid TV
but vast, enormous, spanning the width
of his field of vision from Row Three —
the row, as Marilyn tells him
with a fifth-grader's knowing accent —
where the monsters are in perfect focus.
He cleans his glasses furiously
as the sound track crackles, and a globe
topped with the RKO tower emanates
a zig-zag of Marconi waves, and, lo,
he commences his movie-watching Saturdays
with *King Kong,*[1] who, on that screen,
amid those shrieks and screams of the crowd

---

[1] *King Kong.* This was a U.S. theatrical re-release of a double bill: the original *King Kong* and Val Lewton's *I Walked with a Zombie.*

on-screen and in the audience, strides tall
on his island, taller yet as he scales
the uncountable floors of the Empire State.
He had seen cartoon dinosaurs, but those
who try to wrest the Fay Wray-morsel from Kong
are as real as they get, the first taste
of a primal world of eat-and-be-eaten,
smite-or-be-smitten, the first beware
of the fate of him who falls for Beauty.

An old poet now, on a far coast, he can, if asked,
recite all the names of the movies he saw there
like a litany, week by week, in double-feature pairs,
as dear to him as the saint days to a medieval monk.
A basement full of surgical failures in *The Black Sleep* —
first view of an exposed brain a special thrill.
They do that to crazy people in Torrance, he's told,
skull-top raised up like an egg-cup, brains
poked and stirred around for no more reason
than *Let's see what happens if we do this*.
The mute sad butler played by Lugosi was a pathetic sight;
the man who had been Dracula reduced to a doorman.
Rathbone and Carradine, Tamirov and Johnson
the mad doctor and his henchmen and victims.
This double-billed with *The Creeping Unknown*,
whose alien-microb'd astronaut, gaunt and wandering
assimilates all life in its path: men, cacti and lions,
until it oozes octopoid onto the scaffolding
around Westminster Abbey. Fast work
for stalwart scientist Quatermass who rigs
the metalwork with a million volts
from a nearby power plant.

After *The Blob* he turned inward to his chemistry set
and devised, with his friends, The Boron Monster,
    a bubbling mess
of boric acid, carbonates, and a medley of insect parts
that festered for two days in a Florence flask, then
made a nocturnal exeunt into the floor drain. For weeks
the four boys of the Kingview Science Club swore they heard it
in house pipes and gurgling drains; one went so far

as to say it raised its white pseudopods when he looked
into the late-night toilet bowl.
                              The dreaded Cyclops
from *The Seventh Voyage of Sindbad* seemed as he woke
to stand in silhouette against the bare hill behind his house.
When the garish colors of *Curse of Frankenstein*
reveled in blood and bosoms, he set up shop
in Caruso's garage in Keifertown. *Live Monster Show*,
the hand-drawn poster said in drip-red lettering
and the children came from all around.
Clothesline and sheet for curtain, old 78
of *The Sheik of Araby* a Gothic foxtrot,
his fellow fourth-graders no longer chemists
but grease-paint actors: monster and villagers,
doctor and hunchback. Naturally *he* is the Doctor,
his hands the ones that raise Jell-O brains and send blood
rivulets down the aisles among the screaming girls.
A raincoat, sleeves inverted, can pass for a Dracula cape.
He sends for a mail order course in hypnotism.
They learn the art of mummy-wrapping (green chalk
and Noxzema), black powder and kerosene for fires,
dry ice for malevolent Jekyll-Hyde elixirs.

But there's no keeping up with the Strand and its
accelerating horrors. The bugs have invaded:
ant and tarantula, mantis and locust grown
to the size of locomotives, the dark side
of the atom whose giant flower mutations
they are taught about on schooldays. They would
all glow in the dark and in perfect health
when Our Friend the Atom was done with them.
After *Them!* and *Tarantula*, *Beginning of the End*,
The Giant Claw, and *The Deadly Mantis*,
the worst was *The Black Scorpion*, so horrible,
in fact, that as he watched it open a train
like a sardine can, extract the passengers, then sting
them with its terrible stinger before the slow
ascent to the drooling jaws and mandibles, someone
on the balcony vomited a visual melange
of popcorn and orange soda onto his brother's shoulders.

Then came Godzilla, a whole new order
of urban destruction and radium-breath:
boys who had never seen a city looked on
as power lines and factories, gas terminals and seaports,
glass and steel towers, department stores and palaces
were stamped to splinters and rubble
beneath the wayward reptilian scourge
that had nothing to do with eating: Godzilla was hell-rage,
a force that might wipe clean the earth once and forever
of the human infestation.
                              Godzilla was manifest, too,
in the form of a fat bully on Mulberry Street
who waited to knock the school and library books
from his hands into the nearest snowdrift.
He filled a squirt gun with ammonia and onion juice,
a minor armament since he was studying nuclear fission
and knew a dozen withering curses in Latin.

When the saucers of *The Mysterians* began airlifting women
to help repopulate a dying world, he was jealous,
dreamt of a gravity beam abduction from his own bed.
Forbidden Planet taught him to embrace the alien:
if left on Altair Four he'd happily join Morbius
in solitary study of the long extinct Krell geniuses;
if taxed enough with unjust bullying, he'd join
the crew of Nemo's Nautilus: they'd all be sorry
when he sank half the Atlantic fleet or turned
the submarine to starship and beat the Russians to Mars.
He had never been two towns away,
    but he knew the names of the outer planets' moons.

Small boy in torn shoes and baggy hand-me-downs
sewn from his father's old shirts,
goggle-eyed with wrong glasses, arms full
of comics and all the books he could carry,
he was The Strand's acolyte, its screen and stage
the doorway to a higher reality. No matter
how far he has gone, what written or done,

he is still there, in that seat in Row Three
as the ships land, the invasion commences,
the tentacle comes slowly into focus
at the edge of vision, the branches part
to those two great orbs of The Beast.

He was the one who ran away
    to join the Monsters
        to explore the stars,
haunted, to become the Haunter.

MONDAY, MISS SCHRECKENGOST READS US *LITTLE BLACK SAMBO*

I
We three boys, in the third-grade playground,
one skinny (that's me), one short, and the fat one,
horn-rimmed glasses all, schoolbooks and lunches
in hand-me-down, important-looking briefcases.
We are the serious scholars, the brainiacs —
we know what the ominous Sputnik is beeping
and even why it's there and doesn't fall —
just ask us! We are no good at sports,
try not to be noticed amid the yelling,
the bigger boys' heave and toss of baseball,
football, basketball, whatever ball
it is the season for. We trade our comics,
Superman, Batman, The Flash, Green Lantern,
and offer furtive glances at the forbidden ones,
brain-rotting horror comics some Congressman
has warned our parents to confiscate and burn.
We're saving up to buy sulfuric acid:
a long list of chemistry projects depend
on the pharmacist, Mr. Hoffmann, dispenser
of potions, acids, saltpeter and horehound drops.
"Now, boys," he'd warn us, winking,
"don't go mixing saltpeter with sulfur,
" 'cause that plus a little charcoal is gunpowder.
Don't get yourselves in trouble, okay?"
Oh, no, Mr. Hoffmann, we promise,
we'd never do that, Scouts' honor.
Not one of us is a Boy Scout.

The sun-drenched playground, dark
in the hulking late-day shadow
of the brick schoolhouse, knows fear:
the monthly air-raid sirens, the file
of all of us quickly-quickly-quickly-now
to the basement shelter, the practice
of "duck and cover" in the event of a flash,
a boom and a mushroom cloud

obliterating Pittsburgh on the horizon.
Russkies and Gerries, Japs and Fascists,
Jack-in-the-box Communists
beneath the bedsprings, enemies everywhere.

Monday, Miss Schreckengost, sometime
between geography and "Our Friend the Atom,"
reads an old book to us — you'll like this,
she tells us — it's *Little Black Sambo*.
It even has pictures. The tall boy,
the altogether too tall boy in front row
sinks into his seat. All eyes are on Ritchie,
the Negro boy, held back a year, two years
from the looks of him, too broad of shoulder
to even consider playing with us.
He sits all day where the teacher can mind him.

The story unfolds. Proud little Sambo,
in his new red coat, his beautiful blue trousers,
ambushed by tigers who want to eat him.
He bribes one with his jacket, one with
his beautiful trousers, tricks them to chase
each other head-to-tail round a tree
till they melt to a pool of tiger-yellow butter.
Black Sambo runs home
stark naked to his mother and father,
Black Mumbo and Black Jumbo.

Black Mumbo, who looks like Aunt Jemima,
celebrates with a pancake dinner.
As the book is held up to show its cover
someone calls out, "Hey, that's Ritchie!"
Laughs roil the air like the heat from a veldt.

On Tuesday we added Ritchie Barton
to the list of things to be afraid of.
The downhill road to Caruso's market
became a gauntlet run — the price
of a candy bar was meeting Ritchie's fists.
The older boys, untouchable, caught on,
yelled *Sambo! Look out for tigers!*

from the schoolhouse windows.
Your mama's Black Mumbo!
Your pappy's Black Jumbo!
One day the fifth-grade bully, to our slight relief,
was knocked to the ground before us.

Words thunder	AIN'T
punctuate the blows	NO
as he pounds Timmy	TIGERS
to the pavement	IN AFRICA!
Smaller boys run,	MY MA'S NAME
take the long way home	IS ABIGAIL.
as he pummels Anthony	MY PA'S NAME
against a fencepost	IS SAMUEL.

Fist-crack, nose-break,
tooth-snap, Ritchie's
near-baritone shouts
haunt our dreaming.

II
Miss Schreckengost makes seat assignments
for our field-trip to the hydroelectric dam.
"Forty of us," she counts, "and forty seats."
A kind of chill comes over the classroom.
"Of course we'll draw lots for seat-mates.
You will stay with your seat-mate for the whole trip."

David, the Polish boy, the smallest in class,
is told he will sit next to Ritchie Barton.
At recess, he bursts into tears in the playground.
"I can't sit next to him. I just can't do it."
And I say to Dave, "You're prejudiced.
You're only saying that because he's a Negro."
That ends the conversation.
The one thing no one wants is to be prejudiced.
That's worse than being a Nazi or a Communist.
Dave says, "I just don't want to get beat up."

The day of the trip to Confluence Dam,
the Polish mother keeps her son at home.
Richie sprawls across two seats, feet up,
a clenched right fist slapping an open left palm.
We walk a double-line with seat-mates,
Ritchie alone and trailing far behind,
Miss Shreckengost flamingo-tall ahead of us,
arms pointing at engineering wonders and waterfalls.

I sit in the seat behind Ritchie; Gertrude,
a girl reputed to have head lice,
sits next to me, red pigtails flying.
I have a headache, some dark thing troubling me.
If I'm not prejudiced, I think, then I should sit
in that empty spot beside Ritchie, whose fist and palm
keep time to the road rhythms. All I can see
are noses, teeth, crutches and splints.
I do not want to be beaten, either.

I am not prejudiced.

Years later, I would read in Homer:
More hateful to me than all the gates of Hell
is that man who, holding one thing in his heart,
says another, as I would learn the word *hypocrite*.
Whatever that thing was that I had uttered,
whatever it was called, I was ashamed of it.
I vowed never to do it again.

III
Years later, new town, step-fathered,
we take a family road-trip to Washington.
The parks are filled with picnickers,
families in Sunday whites, blankets and baskets,
matrons with parasols, young couples courting.
They are dressed better than we are,
and there is not one white face among them.
Our angry car passes them, windows up,
doors locked, from Washington Monument
to Lincoln Memorial, a cursory nod

to two Presidents, then off we go
to stepfather's cousin in Maryland.

I remember a handsome, ranch-style home.
I was sent to the living room, turned on
an expensive stereo, where I listened to
the Glazounov Concerto, played by Heifetz.
These must be nice people, I thought.
I went to the kitchen door, listening:

Never seen so many in one place, you say?
They own the city. No decent white
will even go there. In a couple weeks
they're gonna have a Civil Rights March,
a half a million niggers all together,
and that Commie Martin Luther King.
Wish I could get to a rooftop
with this here rifle —
and I know how to use it, too —
wish I could pick him off
and take as many of them with him
as I could, along with those Jew lawyers

I tip-toed back to Russian Glazounov,
       to Jewish Heifetz.

IV
College, and freedom:
"You'll do it with me?" he said, incredulous.
He thought I was joking. I wasn't.
Once I had said *yes*, I had to do it.
I'd done it by then,
with artists, frat boys and athletes,
my notoriety a sure ticket
to never having to ask: *they* asked me.
But no one black had ever asked me.

His basketball arms and legs,
    impossibly long,
        thrust out of his clothes at impossible angles.

An African prince,
    he could snap me in two easily.

"You know what they say about us?"
he asks, teasingly, shirt sliding off.
    I nod.
"It's true. You'll see. No turning back."
His lithe and supple body presses me,
each second more of him
hot against me. I'm shaking.
He pushes me downward,
my hands on his chest
exploring the statue-lines
smooth as marble.
We end up in bed, I'm gasping
against his spent repose. He lets
me examine the palm of his hand,
yes it is lighter there. One rivulet
of pearl-white fluid remains
upon his dark brown forearm.
He puts my mouth there.

It is too quiet. I start to shiver.
I am waiting for the explosion.
"I'm not going to hurt you,"
he assures me. "That was good.
We'll do it again sometime."
He stays a while. I ask
a torrent of questions,
want to know his feelings,
the truth beneath
the hard and proud exterior.

"You want to know
that no one will rent me a room
in this town? Or about the girl,
the white girl who'll only see me
under the bridge at midnight?
Or what they'd do to me
if anyone found out?

Or where I'd be
if I didn't play basketball?"

Just as he's leaving, I say,
"Oh, what's your name?
I'm sorry I didn't ask it."

"Ritchie," he says.
"My name is Ritchie."

OUT HOME

When I was around fifteen, my grandmother, Florence Butler Ullery, decided I was old enough to hear grown-up things. She told me how her father, Albert Butler, had robbed a bank sometime after 1910. He had miscalculated what day the payroll cash arrived, and had come home with only $30 for his trouble, followed within an hour by the police, who dragged him off to jail. She showed me a photo of him — a middle-aged man with a Masonic pin on his lapel — taken in Scottdale, apparently the day he went off to serve his prison term. On the back was written, "The pictures with both of us in them didn't come out. Good-bye from your Pa." He never returned, leaving my great-grandmother Christina Butler, and her children, to fend for themselves.

"Those were rough years, during the First War, and then the Depression came," grandmother sighed. "But folks got through."

Great-grandmother Christina had died four years before, preceded by "Homer," the cigar-smoking old man who boarded with her and to whom it was said she was "secretly married." Homer had presided over one room, piled to the ceiling with cigar boxes, old 78 RPM records and back issues of *Popular Mechanics*. Helter-skelter piles of yellowing newspapers in English and German were hurled out of the window after his death and burned.

My grandmother, a wide-faced, simple woman, sat peeling onions, her chair pulled near the "slop bucket" where the peels fell. "The truth is like this here onion," she said — the first and last time I ever heard her speak metaphorically.

"What do you mean, Grandma?"

She held the onion out for me to examine. It was partially cut open to reveal the white under the skin. "See here — I peeled it and there's the white part." She cut some more. "Now look — there's some dirt and another peel inside." She cut again, halving the onion. "Now the rest is all white. That's the way people talk to you. There's always a lie outside, then a little truth, and then some more lies, and then the inside is all true." She asked me if I understood.

Yes, I said, there were people in town who said one thing and did another. Like my stepfather, "Uncle Joe."

My parents had divorced the previous summer. My mother took up with my father's sister's husband. Two divorces ensued. "Uncle Joe" became my stepfather, proclaiming how happy he was to have such brilliant stepsons and how he would make sure my brother and I got to college. We moved to a new town where nobody knew us, and Uncle Joe and my mother pretended to be married.

One Saturday Uncle Joe came into my room and told me, "You're not welcome here. There will be food on the table, but that's it, since we get child support from your father. The day you graduate from high school, I want you out of here, and don't expect anything from me." I later found out he had dumped his children by a previous marriage in an orphanage some years before. From that time forward, I heard nothing from him except verbal abuse. He condemned me for "sitting around and reading books."

To get away from Uncle Joe and my mother, ("Gertrude and Claudius" in my own Gothic imagination) who were quickly becoming the town drunks, I spent that summer with Grandma, who lived alone now since my grandfather's death. I remember taking Grandma Butler's old rocking chair and placing it under the huge pine boughs, reading Poe and Lovecraft, Dumas and Hugo until it was too dark to see. I had books to read, and woods to roam in, and a quilted bed to sleep in.

A little garden work never seemed onerous, although it hurt to carry heavy water buckets from the nearby spring. The only dreaded chore was emptying the slop pail, which had a tendency to drip on your feet as you stumbled across the lawn with it. When it rained, there was a special task: dragging all the washtubs outdoors to gather labor-free bath water!

Everyone called the four-room house, never completely finished and covered only with black tarpaper, "out home." A coal stove heated the kitchen and a system of pipes and flues heated the other rooms as well. It was snug and warm in winter; in summer, open doors and windows admitted a cool mountain draft, and a lot of chores and food preparation moved to the back porch. There was a dark cool cellar with what seemed thousands of jars of home-canned raspberries, peaches, yellow string beans and apple sauce. Sitting in the kitchen one rainy afternoon, I noticed something I had never seen before. Grandma had a loaded shotgun near the door.

"What's that for?" I asked, alarmed. I was terrified of guns.

"It might be for your Uncle Joe," she said. I smiled at the thought, but assumed she was joking. While my grandfather was alive I had never seen a gun in the house.

The next day, a car came up the long driveway and grandma called me in and told me to turn off the light and duck down in her bedroom. She turned off the television and all the other lights, locked the door, and came into the room and crouched down on the carpet.

I heard the chickens scattering in the yard, then a single set of footsteps on the porch. A light knocking on the door, then louder. Then an angry pounding.

"God-damn it, Florence — I know you're in there! I just want to talk!"

It was Uncle Joe's voice. He must have known I was in there, too, but he didn't call my name. (I can't recall him ever addressing me by my name).

He called "Florence!" one more time, pounded again, cursing. We could hear his angry breath puff out. He stood for a while. He waited; we sat in silence. Then the footsteps tromped down off the porch. There were chicken noises again — a loud one as the rooster went for him and he likely kicked it; anther round of cursing as the rooster followed him to the car; and then the car started up and did the turnaround to retreat back to the mountain road. We waited until everything was quiet again.

"What did he want?" I asked.

Grandmother was livid. She shook with a combination of rage and fear.

"He comes out here, on days when he's supposed to be working. He wants me to go to the courthouse and sign my property deed over to your mother. I told him 'No' twice. I have *three* children and this will always be home for all of them. He wants to use me and your mother to get this house. Your Uncle Ron and Uncle Bob will always have a home here, and your mother too. When Joe comes in the daytime like this, I just turn out the lights and hide."

That night I dreamt of Grandma shooting Uncle Joe dead. It was a good dream.

★ ★ ★

A few days later, while peeling potatoes over the slop bucket, Grandma bent her head toward where the gun stood, and she saw me looking at it, too. She took a deep breath and told me another story.

"My mother — your grandma Butler — lived here for a long time after my Pa went to jail. You don't know what it's like to be a woman in the country, running a house all alone. Your husband's in jail, or in the war, or dies, and there are all these men sitting around in roadhouses reading the paper, and they see the name, and they remember you.

They know you're alone — men you haven't seen since you were a little girl in school.

"One day a car comes up the drive and it's two or three men. They see there's no car in sight, and no man anywhere around, so they get out. They're real polite and respectful. They knock on the door with their hats off. They bring a big sack of groceries. They come in and sit down and have some of your bread. There's a bottle of whiskey in that sack, so they say, 'Let's open it and have a drink.' And you want to be polite, so you get the glasses out.

"And then one of them says something about how lonely it must be out here without a man around. And they laugh and make jokes until you blush. And then they suggest something, and if you had a whiskey with them and you're a little silly and you give in —"

She paused and looked at me, not sure if I, at fifteen, knew what she was saying. I knew. I just looked at her and waited for the rest.

"And if you're dumb enough to do that, then there's no stopping it. They tell their friends, and pretty soon they come by the carload. That's the other reason I keep the shotgun there. That's the kind of thing that happens to ... women."

I had visions of my grandmother — and her mother before her — fending off rednecks with the shotgun, and I never forgot the story.

★ ★ ★

My grandmother Florence has been dead for many years now. Her oldest son Ron, a tall lanky man with speech as slow as melting tar, lived far away and didn't look like anyone else in the family: he's dead too. Her son Bob lived in the house until his passing a few years ago, a recluse. My stepfather, "Uncle Joe," finally moved there with my mother, and gasped his last from emphysema in the run-down shack he had so coveted. The porch sagged in and collapsed. New tarpaper was nailed over the roof while the windows and doors began to rot. My mother is long gone, too, having spent her last years in a high rise where no one had to carry water in buckets from a spring or trek to an outhouse.

Curiosity about Great-Grandma Butler and her Alsatian ancestors led me into some genealogical research a few years ago. I discovered cousins I never knew, and some of them visited the house and sent me photographs. The roof had crumbled and the house was now a ruin. Through the wreckage of the house I could see tattered curtains and the frame of my great-grandmother's bed.

Another photo came a few years later: the land had been sold for taxes and the farmer next door acquired it. Nothing remains of the trees around the house, and of the house, there is now only a slight rise where the foundation and cellar had been.

The cousins interviewed some of the neighbors and found one farmer who remembered all his parents' stories about the Butlers. He knew about the bank robbery, and that Albert Butler was part of a gang of three robbers, all of whom went to prison.

After Albert Butler went to prison, the neighbor farmer reported, Christina Butler supported herself by making and selling moonshine, all through the Prohibition and for some years thereafter.

"Yes, she sold moonshine there," the farmer reported. "But she didn't just sell moonshine. She sold herself — and her daughter Florence."

Truth is an onion. My grandmother, at its white heart, had prepared me to understand it when the time came: "the kind of thing that happens ... to women."

But was it as simple as that: men taking cruel advantage of women?
What did I know about Christina Butler? Once, after sharing a slice of the best bread in the world, fresh from the oven, she showed me a picture of her grandfather, standing in his grape arbor in Alsace. She told me he had been a water-boy for Napoleon on one of his campaigns. "We all loved Napoleon," she told me, "because he overthrew the monarchs." (Napoleon loved his Alsatian troops. He said of them, when questioned about their loyalty: "They speak German, but they *saber* in French!") She died when I was eleven, and as I seldom visited her, I do not remember much else.

More papers came my way, and they were startling. Christina was married twice. First, she had married a man from Lorraine named Georges Jacquillard, who divorced her saying she had committed adultery "with numerous persons on numerous occasions," a charge not contested in the divorce. So Albert Butler was her *second* husband. Had she reformed her ways, or was she in a happy *ménage à quatre* with Butler and his gang members?

It also turns out that the mining towns around Pittsburgh were a hotbed of anarchism in those days. The IWPA was started there and its "Pittsburgh Manifesto" urged violence against capitalists and a maximum of personal freedom for both men and women. "Free love" was one strong component of the movement. Emma Goldman had toured not only Pittsburgh but the coal and coke towns, fomenting radicalism. *Freiheit*, the German-language anarchist newspaper, was everywhere. Was Butler's bank robbery a political act? Did Christina have to make a bonfire of anarchist literature after the failed heist?

Christina practiced "free love," and apparently did so for profit when she had to. And so what should one make of the two men, old "Homer" and my grandfather, who made "honest women" of Christina Butler and her daughter Florence? Homer was a classic recluse, the type of what happens to old anarchists. Who knows what ends their "marriage" served?

My grandfather fit the anarchic mold too: averse to labor to the very end, he lived off "relief" all his days. Once a year, when it came time to pay property taxes, he would trek off, with dread and disgust, to work in a coal mine, but only long enough to raise money to pay the tax bill.

A profound distrust and hatred of politicians prevailed in my grandparents' house, and church-going was treated with mockery. "They dress up on Sunday," my grandmother recalled bitterly, "and they make fun of you for what you wear. And then they talk about you behind your back." I am not even certain that my grandparents were legally married to one another.

These values carried over to my mother, who seemed averse to any public activity. I think she even dreaded going to the post office. I was brought up being told, without explanation, that we were not the kind of people who could go to church, or join things. Not even the Boy Scouts for me. My mother was too simple to be an anarchist: shame seemed to be her driving principle, a desire to live a life in the shadows.

Not one place I lived in as a child remains standing. Yet in my mind I always knew the Diebold-Butler place was there, a last resort and refuge in case the world (or your world) ended. "Out home," you could grow your own corn, tomatoes and radishes, and keep a few chickens. Water always filled the spring, and the rains always came. A "relief" check came once a month, and once in a great while, someone had to go and buy new tarpaper to redo the roof.

At night, you closed the windows tight and a carpet of desperate moths covered the glass on the outside. Whippoorwills echoed back and forth, and, once in a while, something large would lumber through the darkness, making the dogs howl. If you took your name off the mailbox on the road, no one would even know you existed. What you did there, and with whom, was nobody's business. You could wear anything you wanted, or run naked in the woods.

I would not and could not have gone back there, but it will never leave my consciousness. I look at the photographs of the ruined house, with sorrow and loss. Was "Out Home" a derelict hillbilly dwelling, or a self-declared "Temporary Autonomous Zone" for outcasts? Whatever it was, it is gone forever.

THE PINES

Grandmother Butler
grew up with the pines
that dotted her acres.
Her grandpa Diebold
first planted them,
edging the house,
the gravel drive,
the property line.
She watched her daughter
who once could leap
the saplings
grow tall and straight.

Her parents are gone now,
her husband vanished,
her daughters grown and married.
She sits on the porch
and communes with the trees.
Some skirt the house —
she walks soft needle loam
to her raspberry patch —
others trail off and up the hillside.
Squirrels are there in the branches,
black snakes steal eggs
from the hapless robins.
Jays and crows,
cardinals and tanagers
live tier by tier
in their sheltered nests.

Each season a song —
bird twitter spring,
storm hum summer,
cone-drop in autumn,
the groan of trunk
in snapping winter.

They are an orchestra
eternally in tune,
black pyramids at night
against the burning stars,
a comforting wall
against the whippoorwills,
the mountain lions,
the howling winds.

2
One winter day
she's digging down
to the dregs of her coal pile,
filling a pail for the stove,
when a great truck
lumbers in,
piled high with coal.

Two men follow
in a black Studebaker,
tell her they'll dump
as much as she needs —
enough to last her
through widow's winter,
all the way to April.
She hesitates.

They mention her neighbors,
Wingroves and Sweeneys,
Ulleries and Dempseys:
some winters back
they helped them too.

She doesn't answer them;
her head shakes ever
so slightly *no*; the man
exhales an ice cloud,
chilled hands shrugged in
at his elbows. The other
starts up the car to back it
away and out to the road.

"It's just a good neighbor thing,"
he tells her. "The Almanac, it says
it's going to be a terrible winter."
"All right," she says. "Thank you."
She lets them dump coal.
All they want is a signed receipt,
oh, and they'd like
to trim a few trees
for the nearby sawmill.
She hesitates again —
they mumble some words
about another delivery
next winter.

She signs.
Hard winter sets in.
The ziggurat of coal
diminishes to sludge,
black dust in melting puddles.

She goes off in May
to visit her daughters,
hold their new babies.
When she comes back
the pines are gone
    (all but the ones
      that practically lean
      against the house),
reduced to stumps,
her acres exposed
to passing cars,
the rocks
on the bare hill frowning down.

All night the animals
scream in the darkness.
Homeless squirrels,
nestless sparrows
hysterical robins,
even the prowling wind,
with nothing to rub against,

makes angry vectors
among the boulders.

Then she finds the paper
in the kitchen cupboard,
reads with her glasses
the fine print over her signature.
Far off, the ripsaws mock her
as she reads and repeats
what she gave to the stranger —
not just once but forever
    like a contract
        with a rapist,
            her rights, her
                timber rights.

THE BROWN DERBY

Road we don't go down
    weed trees and roadside flowers
shack houses   no toilets
    a collapsed barn
a shingled hall   the Negroes' nightclub
its paint-peeled sign
    THE BROWN DERBY
crowded Saturday
    cars and shouting
sometimes a gunshot   a body
    would float in the creek behind,
    tangled with discarded shoes,
    coal miners' helmets,
    belts and suspenders
    old tires   turtles and crayfish
fished out   dragged to the county morgue
    John Doe'd till someone's son
    was reported missing

Who lives there?   What do they do
on that road we don't go down?
How far does it go?   How many live down there?
Why don't we ever see them
in the school, the bank, the post office?
It's not even on the street map,
    the nameless lane
        of The Brown Derby.

SINKHOLES

i
They called it *The Swamp,*
and although much of the lakeshore
was wetland, weed- and frog-
infested, lily-pad-mosquito-land,
everyone knew, when you said it
with that certain intonation,
voicing italics *and* initial caps,
that you meant *The Swamp.*
It was a pond, reed-fringed
water a shallow cover for floor
of mud from which noxious vapors
bubbled, and where foxfires glowed
on certain moonless nights.
Beneath the mud, though none could see it,
was a water-filled cavern
of unknown depths. I was shown
the Geological Survey map whose legend
denominated a place with no known bottom.

Locals take that on faith:
for generations it's been the place
where useless vehicles, scrap iron
and dead refrigerators are dragged,
pushed with some danger to the townsmen
as they go knee-deep in sucking mud
until their offering is far enough in
for whatever it is that wants things
to begin its inexorable pulling.
Within a day an old jalopy
is nothing but two round headlights,
glass frog-eyes, then nothing
as by the next morning the swamp pool
resumes its perfect flatness, its mud
as uniformly flat as a well-made bed.

ii
I remember a field
we were not allowed to play in —
and playing there anyway
my friends and I discovered
the vertical maw into blackness
we learned was an abandoned mine.
One day it had been a cornfield;
the next the shaft had fallen in.
In a town criss-crossed with forgotten
mines, it could happen anywhere:
holes the size of pancakes, holes
just big enough to swallow a bully,
an arrogant preacher, a rival
(if only one could make them appear!)
Soft ground was best, but even
a sidewalk crack, a storm drain opening,
a gymnasium floor or a toilet
could give way into a sinkhole,
a cenote, a sudden burst
of Karst topography. Someone you really
didn't like could be swept away
into an underground river or fall,
fall, fall beyond the length of rope
to a dull thud at the hard place
between the earth's crust and mantle.

We came back again and again to see it,
to sound out how black
its blackness could measure.
Tar, coal, obsidian, ink: nothing we knew
was blacker than this cavern-hole.
We threw soft coal, and chunks
of sandstone, iron slag
and a 16-ounce soda bottle
as hard as we could from a safe overhang.
No echo answered our probing.
So far as we knew, it had no bottom,
as though the mine below
had been mined *from* below
by subterranean demons.

Although we stopped playing there
and walked a long way 'round
the hillock that humped over it,
in dreams we walked its maw-edge,
lost our bearing, missed one another's
outreached hand of rescue,
or were *pushed* —
and worse by far than the nightmare
of falling into it was the dread
of what might come out of it,
if it wanted to, and was hungry enough.
What if, at night, some shambling Thing
crept into our cellars, filling great sacks
from our coal bins, returning the fuel
to the mountain depths? What if we went,
as we sometimes did, to stoke the furnace
at the stroke of midnight
and came eye to eye with *It*?

iii
I read of places
where sink holes appear
without warning, some watered
beneath with underground rivers,
but others just chasms, cave vents
or rifts between two angry seams
of geologic tension. Cybele's
temple was just such a place,
its altar an opening into darkness
that drove women mad, and men
to self-mutilation.
Just such a place
is the entrance to Tartarus,
nine days below Hell.

One falls, not into open space
like Milton's bad angels
(who enjoyed a feast of starlight
while they plummeted) —
but no, one falls
    into an ever-narrowing funnel

   of cold darkness,
into a place where legs
   and arms are useless
until there is nothing of you
   but a head screaming upwards
towards an ever-dwindling
   pinpoint of light.

Our earth is a shifting island of sea and magma,
Swiss-cheesed with sink holes, cenotes,
Blue Holes at the bottoms of coral seabeds —
Something riddled with Nothing,
orbiting a self-regulated explosion,
sun hurtling around and away from
the Black Hole at the rift of space-time,
Every moment of existence here averts
an infinity of empty, unpeopled stars.

THE BUTCHER KNIFE

Not once did I see one used for butchering:
the wooden handle firm in the grasp,
the broad, long edge, serrated ominously,
quite capable of rending limb from torso,
or a small head from a shuddering spine.

No, the fame of these kitchen implements
was their use by neurotic aunties,
stepmothers too jealous and easily provoked,
old wives at the end of married tether.

Medea in slippers and terrycloth,
red-eyed from onion chopping,
she waved it aloft in a shrieking rage, or,
worse by far, swung it in stone-eyed silence.

She could chase and corner a terrified
stepchild (while her own, better daughter
watches from the stairwell landing),
or send the man hurtling to corner tavern.

In the right hands, this most domestic
of kitchen tools clears any house
of inconvenient relatives,
of the need for cooking and mending,

a Pennsylvania Gothic sword
that never needs sharpening.

WHAT'S IT TO ME

What's it to you? a neighbor asks me.
Why write about Germany, Poland,
the struggling masses of Russia?
Who cares? We're all Americans now.
Why you of all people, with that fine English name?

English is but part of what I am,
and even that is outsider,
Nothumberland and border Scot.
Three ancestors beheaded
at the Tower of London,
rebels against the throne,
so don't imagine me
on the Queen's Christmas list.

As for the maternal side
count me a Theobaldus
    Thibault in France
    Diebold in Alsace
Vosge mountain village
from which we heard the call
to serve Napoleon
    and answered
(young Diebold a water boy
at the Emperor's own tent).

We fled Alsace
to escape the Prussians
    who killed an old woman
    for calling a *kartofel*
    a *hard apfel*,
traded the sweet Vosges
for the wild Appalachians

Cousins back home
    endured the Prussians,
    celebrated reunion
        with France,
    and then endured the Nazis.

Under the German Reich,
Alsace became Elsass again.
All the young men
    were drafted for infantry,
sent to the Eastern front
to fight the Russians.
Most died, but thousands
    were captured.
They never came home.
Unwilling "Germans,"
they died in Stalin's gulag.

Oh, it's personal.

ALL I KNOW ABOUT MY FATHER

When someone asks *Your father?*
I conjure a blank, a void,
a vacant place at table, in heart,
a self-erasing memory.
Sometimes I envy poets
who sift from out their childhood days
a paradigm moment,
a passing of wisdom,
a graceless hug,
eye twinkle of reflected pride.
I try, and come up empty.

Once, in the living room,
he showed me places on a globe;
I glimpsed
in closely guarded scrapbook
a ruined, barbed-wire Europe
whose ovens had singed him.
He had a German medal.
Arbeit, it said.
He showed me the tanks,
the marching columns
in which he'd tramped,
GIs like chessmen
riding and walking
filling the map
to meet the Red chessmen,
pawns in the mine and yours
diplomacy of Yalta.
I still recall their farmboy faces,
the broken walls behind their pose.

Once we walked on a slag pile.
He hurled things angrily —
sticks, rocks and bottles —
into a quicksand pool.
I think he meant to tell me something:
There is a place that draws you to it.
There is a force that sucks you under.

There is a way to walk around it.

Days he kept books at the belching coke ovens,
debits and credits in the sulfurous air;
nights he played jazz at roadside taverns.
One night we even heard him on the radio.

I tried to play his clarinet — just once.
He yanked it away.
Daily and nightly the man was there.
Thirteen years of a father
who wanted a room between himself and sons.
So this is all that I remember:

He was the voice who fought with my mother.
He slept on the couch, then in another house.

Years passed, birthdays and Christmases
unmarked and unremembered.
When I was seventeen he phoned the school,
said he would meet me at the top of the hill.

I walked there, wondering
what we might have to say,
what new beginnings —

Sign this, he said.
What is it?
*A policy. Insurance we had
on you and your brother.
I'd like to cash it in.*
I signed. The car sped off.
I never told anyone.

When someone asks *Your father?*
I shrug. He is an empty space,
a vacuum where no bird can fly,
a moon with no planet,
an empty galaxy
where gravity repels
and dark suns hoard their light.

ENGLISH BREAKFASTS

i
Grandmother died yesterday,
a little girl tells me at breakfast,
and Mommy says we'll inherit something.
How English, I think.
The teapot hides
in a quilted cozy.
The sugar is cubed,
the silver spoons polished
by the Irish maid.
Not one pinched face at this table
can extrude a tear.

ii
On the street, a moving truck
is engorged with furniture.
Its double-doors close.
A thin, pale woman
looks back at the Tudor
house, the round hill,
the enclosing oaks.
I suppose I shall miss it,
she tells her husband.
It had too many rooms, anyway.

They drive off. The house
settles and sighs audibly.
A branch falls
from an embarrassed maple.

iii
My father, whom
I had not seen in thirty years,
told me of his memories:
Your grandfather took me out
for a beer once.
I was twenty-six
and in the army.
It's the only time
he ever really talked to me.

When I wrote, I called him "Old One."
He signed his letters,
"Don."
Going on sixty, I warmed up
to "Venerable Rutherford";
he was past ninety,
and, finally, at the close
of a hand-printed letter,
he ended it:
DAD.

THE BLUE BOY

On certain Sundays I was sent alone
to the apartment on Pittsburgh Street,
its mothball and camphor-smelling hallway
cool in the steep ascent, the dim window
into an airshaft a curiosity, the knock
on glass-paned inside doorway, the wait
as slippered feet padded slowly, as the brass

knob turned and the small frail figure
of Olive Rutherford peered out,
pretended surprise, and her calm voice said,
as always, "You've come for tea, and cookies."
Sweet oven smells, and cinnamon
flooded out to greet me. She had an air
of lilac and smothered roses.

The parlor was small,
the sofa seat so high my short legs dangled
as I waited for the tea tray, the fine white teapot,
the delicate curved cups, the cubed sugar,
the milk I always declined and wished she woudn't
fill to precarious brim in a silver pitcher.

"So nice that you prefer tea," she always began.
"So civilized." "Coffee," I'd say, "is for barbarians.
I tasted it once when I was five — enough that once
for a lifetime." She asked what I was reading, I rattled
off authors and titles: Dumas and Dickens,
last week two science fiction books: Van Vogt
and Merritt. She nodded at the classics, looked down
at the science-fiction names, said not a word
at the *Superman* comics I held on my lap.

To my mere ten, she seemed a thousand years old.
I wondered whether she slept, and what
she did in all the days of her solitude
(husband dead for thirteen years now).

The one bright thing in this mummy parlor
was the immense portrait on the wall
that seemed to glow with its own power.
Gainsborough's "Blue Boy," she told me,
painted in 1770, so loved in London
that ninety thousand persons lined up
to view it for one last time
when a California millionaire bought it.
It was not the original, of course, but a copy —
to my small eyes as large as life. The boy,
in those clothes, would be bully-taffy
from here to the schoolyard: arrayed in blue
against the dim green background of elms
and willows, he almost stepped
from canvas into the parlor.

His silk blue suit, trimmed in silver;
his dangling wide hat, outrageously feathered,
would be torn to shreds in minutes,
the petulant pout and his lips, his large,
soft eyes, doe innocent, his runaway curls
and quiff of raven hair suggest the friend
you'd like to have but would need to protect;
but the half-cape twirled on one arm
reveals a gracefulness, the ease
of incipient swordplay, the legs
in their tight bindings well-made
for running. I looked at my shoes,
featureless leather with string laces:
his, impractically, are tied in bows.
Hard to imagine how he dressed himself:
no Boy Scout, but a pampered aristocrat.
No one in my family possessed or wore a suit.
"Is that how they dressed in 1770?"
"He painted the boy in antique costume."
my grandmother explained. "That's what
a nobleman's son of *1670* would wear.
That's what makes paintings interesting,
riddles inside of riddles to the mind."

This is all that I remember of her: book talk
and tea. Secrets she had: she had borne
ten children. Her mother, it was whispered,
was a Mingo Indian. She had outlived
the rise and fall of the coke ovens, the mines,
the giddy little empires of bank and ruin.
Perhaps she told me things I have forgotten:
all tea becomes, with time, but a single cup.
Half-there, is a memory: on an aunt's
porch glider, she told me strange syllables
she said were the secret names of animals.

Three years later I saw her casket,
peered at her still-jet-black hair, her
Indian nose and cheekbones, smelled
the last hint of lilac.

Cape on one arm, broad hat
outrageously feathered,
silk tunic and leggings trimmed in silver,
a pale boy stood opposite.
I nodded, the only one
to see him, silent as mine
his last respects.

AT THE FUNERAL HOME

My mother, behind me,
pushes open the door
to the funeral parlor.
"Go in," she says,
"and sign the book.
Pay your respects
to your grandmother."

Not sure what that means
except in movies, I enter
the dim vestibule: a slanted table,
a large book opened
to "Olive Rutherford."

I sign. Tall men in suits
and women I've never seen before
move in and out of another room.

I follow. I am drawn,
though I do not wish to be,
to the casket. My steps
become protracted, smaller,
as though infinitesimal
inchings would never get there.

I look around for uncles and aunts:
there are ten of them, a horde
of cousins I've never met.
My father, who seldom spoke
to his mother, is absent,
gone since the double-divorce
and scandal.
No sign of his sister, Margie.
No sign of Uncle Bill, the newsstand owner.
The others I have never met.

These are all strangers. If Rutherfords,
they ignore this adolescent Rutherford
as I approach the dread casket.
There, gaunt as ever, hair black
as a raven's quills, her Indian nose
and high cheekbones, hands crossed,
some rose and lily petals tossed
hazardly here and there around her,
there, is Olive Rutherford.
I don't remember make-up:
they have made her phosphorescent.
Her pursed lips preserve their secrets,
the things I should have known
when I was old enough. What interval
passes as I stand there, I do not know.
I have never seen a dead person before.
Like this, I think, *beneath the ground
and forever.*

I feel like a chimneysweep
among these dressed-up people.
Snatches of talk pass over me:
"I don't suppose she left you
anything." "She owned two buildings."
"We'll not be staying for the funeral."
"Her late husband, the old Burgess,
a wonderful man. We all miss him."

No one speaks to me. No one comes forward
to ask who I am. I tip-toe backwards,
back to the dark vestibule, out
to the winter sunlight, to the car,
where my mother, no longer Rutherford,
waits with eyes turned downward.
Our car, the right rear door held on
with rope, slinks out of Scottdale.
Except for last respects we have
no business being here.

TO MY STEPFATHER

I have your ashes before me. Too bad
the worms did not get their turn with you.
But thanks to cremation, a classic end
to a dreadful and drunken existence,
I can carry what's left of you easily
on my coming trip to Avernus, where
I will bribe the tour guide for a night's stay
in the cave behind the ruined temple,
where I will find, in a lambent moonbeam,
the rock crease I read about; and I will grasp it,
and the stone wall will indent and turn, as it did
for Aeneas; and I will descend the staircase,
one step for every hundred years of man
into the utter darkness, until I hear
the black roar of the Stygian river.
I will calm the hell-hound, pay
to the boatman his requisite coins,
lull him with poems as he tirelessly rows
(time enough for an epic, I am sure.)

And when the dead come to greet me,
surprised that a stepson should accompany
your still-disintegrated remnants,
I shall wave them away, wave back
the long line of your ancestors, eager
to learn of your life and its doings.
I shall astonish them with my demand
to be shown the nethermost cave,
whose mouth gapes black into the inky,
ebony darkness of Tartarus —

for if the Hell of the Dead
is ten days' falling from the bliss of earth,
Tartarus is ten days' more descent,
ten times remiss of light, and warmth,
and love. I do not know what guardian
I'll find at the great iron gates —
some heartless son of Pluto or an angry

Titan from the Hundred-Handed Host —
but I will find the word and the key
so that I pass the barrier of Zeus.
If anyone can do this, a poet can:
for are not half the gods our own
inventions, brought into life
by the wish-will of words invoked?

Whatever flame and peril await me
in the atom-lock cold of Tartarus,
I shall carry this urn, past the dread brow
of Saturn and his gnawing hunger,
past the icy palace of oak-queen Rhea
with its methane auroras and acorn domes,
past the eternal wrestling match
of the hundred-handed slayers of gods,
past all those horrors and more will I go,
for I know my duty (your ashes down
before your spirit's own slow migration):
to find the drearest, bottom-most place,
the cesspit of universal waste and carnage,
the place from which no resurrection comes,
from which rebirth is inconceivable,
and there, in a black pool, I will spread
your ashes, stepfather, as I swore,

so you will crawl, a blind slug in a swill
of beer foam and tobacco, whiskey and sawdust,
the vomitorium of the most-cursed gods.
And here, from time to time, you may meet
your own kind, fanged as you are
for mutual consumption, loined as you are
for the sterile pleasure of fornicating
in a sea of hydrofluoric acid. Then I will leave
the urn and wend my way calmly upward,
a pinpoint of light before me, year by year
expanding to the great blue sky of stars.

MR. PENNEY'S BOOKS

Bay-windowed room in gingerbread Victorian,
bookshelved from floor
to cast-in-shadow ceiling —
my dream of my own retirement-exile, to be
left alone at last amid ten thousand
books, and cabinets whose sliding drawers
concealed vast sheaves of etchings, prints,
treasures way back to incunabula days.
And the room — it was Mr. Penney's —
with its great desk and drawing board
tack-pinned with unfinished blueprints
of a magnetic perpetual motion engine —
was itself a mere anteroom
to corridors and attics, niches
and passageways, book
upon book, a hollowed hive
of unkempt learning.
It was here, as a high-school boy,
I came for my *real* reading:
Voltaire and Paine and Ingersoll,
the little Blue Books of skeptical thought,
the slim red classics of Everyman's Library,
the histories piled high 'mid Verne
and Conrad, Tolstoy and Maupassant.
Each day I'd listen rapt to his tales
of selling Vermont marble
in post-earthquake San Francisco
of his newspaper days,
dragging O'Henry from drunk-bar
to his deadline desk, long years
of teaching young men the rigors
of mechanical drawing; of buildings
designed and constructed (he'd built
one of the first automat restaurants);
of patents granted and sold too cheap.
Eight decades had crept upon him; he joked
"I never dreamt I'd live to the day
that I grew tits, and my wife a beard."
Sons and grandsons tramped the big house,

not one of them a reader. Each week
his son's wife heaped Penney's books
into the curbside trash-can; each week
he was up before dawn-crack to retrieve them.
Hundreds were the volumes he gifted me.
"You'll read them. What's more, you'll pass the gift."
I nodded, books piled to my chin, tottered home.
I read three a day then,
as though I had come to books from a desert,
or dreaded returning to one.

        Gone from home,
gone to school, gone to the city, I have
a dim memory of someone mentioning
"Old Mr. Penney died a while back."

I made one final visit to the hated town,
raked my stepfather'd house of every scrap
of my existence there: old manuscripts,
my few remaining comics, cartons of books
I had left behind for someday-retrieval.
My mother, between beers and cigarettes, said:
"Oh, the Penneys came by one day. They said
he left you all his books. We were
going to write you a letter,
but then I never found a stamp,
and I guess I lost the envelope."
My mind screamed *What?!* —
my voice went novocaine,
a tiny "Oh," my only response.

Friend's car packed up
with all my juvenilia, I asked,
"Let's turn left here. There's a house
I want one last remembrance of."
We slowed to stop. Three people rose
from their porch chairs, swung wide
the double stained-glass door.
The porch light flickered, failed.
Inside, the door to Mr. Penney's library
was thrust open, then slowly shut

like a drowsy eyelid. An arc
of hall-light swept over the floor,
over and across to the deep bay window.
Bare floors, bare walls, stark corners,
bookless, shelfless, deskless and desolate,
then dark as the door closed. The hall's
lights went black, unlettered Penneys
ascending their crisp, clean, dustless stairs
to sleep. We drove off
without speaking, our car trunk full,
back seat piled high to the tipping point
with all the books I'd ever owned.

love spells

WHEN DID I KNOW

When did I know
that I was the thing they don't speak of,
whose nicknames even were unprintable?
Was it all the way back
at school's beginning, when I knew
and could name the prettiest girl
in answer to my mother's *Who
would you marry?* but didn't tell
that I could also rank the boys
in tiers of beauty, had anyone asked?

So many moments, so early:

When a boy cousin jumped on top of me
and said *Let's play husband and wife* —
twelve going on thirteen I had no idea
what that meant, except
it was the first time anyone touched
who wasn't hitting me. Even through clothes
the feel of flesh on flesh made me tremble.

When my best friend, wrestling
me down on my narrow bed, asked
Why do you always let me win?
and I couldn't answer.

When I stopped being alone, ever,
with my grandfather, who,
whiskered in his long underwear
would try to pin me down
with sadistic tickling on any day
the women were out of sight.
Because the body is a poem, mine
for my use and not another's, mine
to discover its willing partner.

When boys and girls huddled
hushed in a backyard tent,
a new game with much at stake,
showing their forbidden parts
by flashlight, I looked away
at the girls' turn, then lay awake
remembering the slow unzip
of the boys' trousers.

When one of the girls
it was dangerous to know
contrived a dozen ways
for me to walk her
through lonely places, woods,
even the night-time graveyard,
and I was a gentleman always.
(And when another, heaped
against me on the dance floor,
finally blurted despairingly,
Don't my breasts interest you?)

When, as a seventh grader
on the first day of school I watched
in mingled horror/fascination
as senior boys emerged
from the gym class showers,
and then I dreamt of dark caverns
or a secret-passage attic
where all of them,
in an endless state of dressing,
undressing and self-caressing
lined up in an A to Z roll call,
slaves of my eyes' hunger.

When I watched one after another
Godzilla and Toho monster films
and could not take my eyes off —
no, not the lumbering, costumed
monsters — but Japanese men,
young ones, hard-cheeked,
dark-eyed and raven-haired,
an urge I could never plummet
to sated boredom.

And why, when I learned
that some men were otherwise inclined,
did my mouth not utter, ever,
the expletives? Surprised, delighted
even, each clue and glimmer
of a kindred species like a key shard,
a piece to be joined with other pieces
until the rainbow bridge could be completed,
my exit up and out of this
world I did not belong in.
If there had been a place to go
to meet them, I would have gone there.

But most of all is that starburst
explosion when you find the one face,
the one accepting glance, the one
surrendered night when all is given,
all asked-for taken with joy,
to know that the love given here
is as cosmic as any force in the universe,
to want and to be wanted by the same person.

I never asked to be normal.
Always and ever,
    for as long as I can remember
I was not like the others,
and the joy-quest yearning
was to find others
    equally blessed, equally scorned.

The names they call us
    were nothing compared to the golden vowels,
    the sibilants, the fluted song-tones
        by which we would greet one another.

Somehow,
    in the dark of nightside passages,
and in the intervals of daylight
they grant us, we find our own,
either the fervent flesh-touch
of youth to youth, or the helping
hand of our elder kind, the lift
and repair of wings broken, hopes
dashed by the limits of mortality.
We have our own biology and history.
Our children are the things we make,
our fossils the Trilobites of culture.
Some want us dead and gone, but
try to imagine the world without us.

IRISES

Before a certain bridge I cross each night —
my eyes are bent downward so as to miss
who does or doesn't come to that window —
I study a cottage's garden plot.
I have never known who lives here,
but have grown to know that militant line
of soldier irises in purple plumes,
their wind-rumpled hoods on defiant spear-ends,
the constant bulbs as certain as sunrise.

By day the flowers welcomed visitors —
hived bees and humming, brazen dragonflies,
by day they shamed the variable sky.
(By day I see that, in your nearby loft,
your windows darken,
concealing your presence or your absence.
Only your door mouth, opening and closing,
admitting and ejecting visitors,
confirms to me that you are tenant still.
Your lovers' faces smite me with smiling;
in their dejection I recall my pain.)

On moonless nights I man the silent bridge,
brood on the madness of water lilies
that choke up the swelling, algae'd outlet.
I peer over the dam-edge precipice
at the shallow, tamed creek bed far below.

Beneath the lit and curtained windows
of your unsuspecting neighbor,
the irises stand guard like sentinels,
dark eyes awatch beneath those still petals,
the hidden golden stamens scolding me,
the patient bulbs oblivious to love,
serene as Buddhas, requiring nothing.

Within your casements,
above the dim-dark bookstore,
a galaxy stirs,
a sphere of light in a candle centered,
then other spheres, then moving silhouettes.
One is your cameo, then you are lit.
Moving to music now, your arms might close
around another's neck. Your visitor
eclipses you, his night enfolding you,
your ivory breast his evening star,
his your heartbeat till morning's dim crescent.
(O double Venus, which of you is true?)

Lights out, all but the streetlamps,
I turn back to my sleeping irises,
black blooms in owl-watch, consoling friars.
All day you give me eyes-alms blossoming;
all night you silently companion me,
never mocking this madness of loving,
dying of perfect beauty, and alone.

THE OBSESSION

But one man loved the pilgrim soul in you,
And loved the sorrows of your changing face.
          W. B. Yeats, "When You Are Old"

Of him whom I loved the first and best,
I have left so much unspoken.
Hundreds of pages I might have filled,
thousands the images comparing him
to every icon of classical beauty.

Instead I waited for the calm reflection,
beamed back from the pool of the mind.
Night cannot know the sun will follow,
    nor the road, the conquering weed,
    nor the truth of love, the worm inside it.
The outcomes to love-me, love-me-not
    are either-or, or neither-nor,
or the side-slough of the reaper's blade.

Sleepwalking, amnesiac, self-hypnotized
to forget him, all I could do
was fill every niche, imago, daemon
with his eidolon. Absence
and presence were coin-sides
of his continued existence.
Only his death
empties the witch-pot of wanting,
and even then his face floats upward
in the steam cloud of soul's diaspora.
I reach — my hand comes back
cold, wet, and empty — a name
can no longer summon him.

I have had a sole thought,
unpublished except between us,
in the sombre purity of detached years —
a gold and lapus scarab
untarnished in the pyramid of time:

it moves my pen, my haunted eye,
defies my age's forgetfulness,
a swan's lament suspended, held.

If it be not sung, this
perennial ode of too-few notes, or one,
which I would say in full but that
he and the sun take it away from me
and one of us comes not back —
if it be not sung at last,
    my soul, it dies with me,
nor I nor the world larger for it,
nor he, moved neither to hear
    nor answer it
on his dark journey downward
to the black waters.

The memory of first-seeing:
he sat at the perfect center
    of grace and beauty.
Around him the songs of divas
cast a protective veil. We hovered
in breathless empathy, like courtiers,
around his darkened room, cowed
before a pair of expensive speakers,
a turntable no hands but his
were allowed to touch,
as Streisand twisted
from comedy to bluesy darkness —
as Piaf chanson'd herself to death for love
of the boxer, the convict, the forlorn
and nameless man *qui me suive
dans la rue,* for the cruel one,
Milord Death who sat at her café table —
Inca Yma soaring four-octaves high
in wind song of Andean lament.
And then suddenly, a dash of Horowitz,
or the shriek-scrape of Edgard Varèse,
all this so different from my world
of Beethoven, Mahler, and opera.

His magic was in making it seem
that every love song had him
as its only object, and that we,
each moth and mite of us,
were doomed to circle him
as that last arc on a long playing record
when the needle leaves the fade out
to final orbit, imprisoned us
in heart-thump going-nowhere.
Then, every night, like closing time
at a tavern for doomed men,
there came the palpable silence
of no more music, our talk exhausted;
our clumsy withdrawal, as one by one
we are not chosen, each home
to a single bed and a shared despair.
If this had been the Renaissance,
dirks might have been drawn
in a darkened alley, poisons purchased
to eliminate all rivals; love poems hurled
into and through his window casements.
His tribute came in dark-shadowed eyes,
mumbled confessions or silent hatred,
the red ribbon of a slit wrist.
What spider stratagem was this?

I did not play the game, I thought.

I could go home to my own
gods and divas: Nilsson in Wagner
or the high art of Wanda Landowska
in Bach's Forty-Eight, a realm
in which he seldom tread.
I watched the moth-dance of his admirers
as from an amused distance,
and told him so.
"I know you know," he told me,
"and that is why I respect and fear you."

I could withdraw at night's end
and with a Shakespearean flourish
end all with a rhymed couplet,
cool, Platonic, a cipher on Attic marble.

Beneath, I was *Sterminator Vesevo*.[1]
I never told him that every sight
of him threw me vertiginous
to the edge of a lava flow.

He thought he had no place in these poems,
the making of poems a mystery to him,
as the making of his sculptures was to me,
the poem a thing inside, too many words
reduced to a few; the sculpted figure
an immanence inside a block of stone
the removal of all that was inessential.
I shuddered each time I touched
    a thing he had made;
perhaps my poems were like fire to him,
a thing too fierce to be endured.

Though he was not my brother-listener,
I learned from him that I do not write alone,
In the moment I confessed to myself
that I loved him, I saw in full light
what Beatrice was to Dante, Lara to Zhivago,
the loved boy to Hafiz the madman.
He would not take the light I offered.
I even feared he would not take it from others —
some joy for me, at least, if he were loved
    as I loved him.

Full many nights we courted, flirted,
    word-circled one another.
One night our talk outlasted
    the guttering candle.
That night, he came to my bed —
    O summer night of which I cannot speak —

---

[1] *Sterminator Vesevo*. Exterminating Vesuvius, the name given to the famous volcano by Italian poet Giacomo Leopardi.

almost to curse me by a single giving
of what he pretended so slight a gift
as to forget it ever happened.

Gone to the city, I dreamt of him still,
    knowing only the where and how of him,
    not writing, not calling.

One night, uncannily, he phoned me.
I could hear, in the background, the Bach
Toccata, Aria and Fugue[2]
on his phonograph. "It made me think of you,"
he said. At the very same moment, I swear,
I was playing the same music, the same
Carnegie Hall Horowitz forever linked
in my mind with nights at his side.

I refined, from shattered bits of him,
    a spirit he did not possess
    a voice and charm
    he never intended to give me.
He had no inkling what children we birthed!
Here in my wordy palace his regency's intact—
    back on drear earth,
discarded lovers conspired against him,
moths in his aurora,
graying the New England autumn
where he went to teach,
or bleaching to graveyard white
the coral reef beyond his final place of hiding.

Did he fear me to the end? My harmless love-lie
trapped him only in the realm of angels
where immaterial ghosts of me
came to call, masked, and offered dangerous prizes.

---

[2] J.S. Bach's *Toccata, Aria and Fugue in C* was originally for organ. Horowitz recorded the haunting piano arrangement of it by Ferruccio Busoni.

I waited for seven years.
We met, collided, repelled like angry magnets.
I was ready, at last, to admit defeat of pride
and offer self and art at his idol.
After one night of passionate embraces
no more were offered. Visiting his friends,
all cheerfully living with tormented boyfriends,
he said in the car afterwards, "I don't want
to be thought of as part of a couple." "Oh," I said,
and traced my way home to New York in desolation.

That sealed our vow
of mutual avoidance.
Once in a great while I received
    a polite letter;
once in a great while I sent
imprudent poems, my pride and solace.
They circled him like great white owls,
summoned him to the dark wood of my waiting.

Now they have told me of his death,
which culminates at last the thing between us.
I return to the place of our meeting.
I am here in autumn pilgrimage,
back to the silent, pebbled lakeshore.
I wait, uncloaked, beneath a gibbous moon,
chilled as the damp fog enfolds me.
I have no promise of ghosts, or of Heaven,
no cause to hope that some thread, tenuous
and febrile as thought in ether, might draw
him here, eyes to my eyes, mind to my mind,
touch to my touch, companioning. So much
unfinished business between us, too few
the decades of life in which to do it. All
the wrong people keep dying, I tell myself.

I had thought we would meet but one more time,
as calm old men over tea and remembrances.
Here at the lake of our college town,
I touch the limestone with its fossil memories.
I taste the water, breathe in

the hovering mist, the bat and maple aura
of the town settlers' graveyard. Some single blossom,
complex and curled upon itself
like a tropical orchid,
drifts silently toward me in the black water,
while the wind and waves sing Bach's *Aria*.

Know this as the place of my waiting.
That my waiting will outlive me,
repeated as some other stands here
and reads aloud these words, the vow
of solitude and folly
I made some thirty years ago:

Know I will wait,
      that I am bound,
           that no other has ever been awaited
                or will be.

A YEAR AND A DAY

A year since last I saw you. No: a year and a day.
The round red sun struck an octave falling,
rung out the interval as turning earth
returned to the self-same place in its orbit:
and what should happen, but nothing at all.
Nothing, or rather, another day void
to add to a year of days without you,
the same fields dressed up in the same green trees,
the same indifferent sky accepting bursts
of egomaniacal seedpods
attempting escape velocity.

During the year, I fled the quotidian,
twisting with maple propellers,
out and upward to the highest cirrus.
I sought the place of your waiting
somewhere in orbit beneath the Dog Star.
All too soon I fell, repelled
by a single graze of your cheekbones.

I thought the sun, unbent by atmosphere,
would melt your cold heart;
the rain that came
we mistook for a sign of advent —
o roots, o tendrils, o new shoots twining,
abandoned as abruptly
to summer's drought,
to hoarfrost cold,
and now, to this barren anniversary.

Each height I sought
you had already abandoned.
Each bloom thrust up —
whether the frail violet
    or the tight-fisted peony —
beautiful to me only
in some resemblance, passing,
to some aspect of you,

fell petal by petal to cindered ash.
Earth's autumn hecatombs
were burned in vain at your altar.
I know you were always there,
just one horizon beyond me,
hurrying on, pursued, and pursuing
(I dread to name whom or what!)

Must I follow you to desert rim,
the unforgiving edge of the glacier,
the *Mere de Glace* where Monster
and Maker (for what else are lover
and beloved?) meet once,
soliloquize and part, sworn enemies?[1]

For a year and a day you have fled me —
(Ah! it is a year and a day, times thirty now!) —
and still the secret lives, as flowers shriek
in fields the winds italicize with longing,
in wan birch forests that topple and fall
at your departing slant. The secret lives;
the long count of calendar days resumes,
and we (myself and all things living)
tread on in quest of that one contrary wind
that would be harbinger of your return.

I will not die waiting, but you will wait
'til your own death to plumb regret's full sea.
Green things will bloom, mute, melancholic, doomed,
beneath a kettle of iron-gray storm-clouds.
Life will go on somehow, though gods are fled
and I, of words and love, am but a ghost.

---

[1] *Mere de Glace.* The scene on the glacier where Victor Frankenstein is confronted by the Monster in Mary Shelley's *Frankenstein*.

WHAT SHE WAS LIKE

In October, he was home to stay.
Last night, as chill November ripped
the last red remnants from the maples,
and Orion stalked the horizon
he told her, "Mother,
I have to leave. I am returning
to Florida. I can't explain."

It was all he could do to get the words out.
In a month he had not said a thing
of what he had to tell her.
He had called no one, content
to be driven to malls and dinners,
polite teas with her old friends
who had never been permitted
to forget his existence, though he
saw them all as a blur of old shoes,
primped hair in unnatural hues,

coats too many times out and back
to cold storage. Tanned and plump
he felt like an exotic parrot
in a town full of mummies.

They made a striking pair.
She was a beauty once, her line
    of noble cheek and chin
as proud as his own; nature
kept all her hair, and artifice
kept it black as ever, while his
had long receded, speckled with white.
Still, she carried herself well,
as if afloat above her shoes,
as if afflicted still
    with fatal allure
(once his own curse, and power).
She is Lady Madeline Usher
to his Dorian Gray.

"The cab is on its way," he tells her
as they make morning motions
upstairs, downstairs.
She does not protest. One sigh,
head droop and hand-drop
says everything: out of her sight
is out of existence. His butterfly
would fade to moth memory.
Once more, he'd be reduced
to an object of conversation:
Art school — No, never married,
poor boy — lives far away.
I've never met his friends.
Perhaps, from there, from the safe
distance of a letter, he could tell her.

As he packs the last suitcase,
reverse motion from a month ago,
things won't fit easily.
"You have scarcely time for breakfast,"
she admonishes from the doorway.

"I'd rather shower," he says.
"You have so many things now,"
   she says, alluding
   to all her recent gifts,
"impossible to pack them all.
This is so sudden."

Most of the clothes are in the closet.
They are dead weight, ballast
to keep his ship from sailing.
Just one new suit, an exquisite black,
he folds beneath old jeans,
his khaki trousers and well-worn shirts.
It would have its use.

She mumbles something, it sounds
like "Oh, very well." She's gone.
He takes a towel and razor and soap
for his hurried shower — and then —
as though in dream's slow motion
he passes her bedroom where

two disembodied arms stretch out,
   two alabaster cylinders
   arms odalisque, surreal,
against a paisley bedspread —
no, it is a mirror laid flat on the bed,
   reflecting two arms to the elbow bared,
the door ajar, as she intended it;

he peers round to see her thrashing there,
   half-crouched, a butcher knife
before her transfixed eyes, first
   in one hand, then tightly in two,
the one-hand gesture a throat-cut sweep,
   two-handed, it turns upon herself,
   blade pointed at base of bosom,
   a disemboweling thrust if only
she would — but she doesn't.
   She looks up, sees him seeing her.
The door goes shut.

He tiptoes past, decides
    he will forego the shower.
With a great motion
    he did not think within him,
he rises, bags in both hands —
neither embrace nor handshake
a possibility as he backs
down the stairway and down
to the door; it opens somehow
behind his fumbling fingers
twisted as they are with bag-holds,
and he is out.

The full light of cloudless day,
out there, the oxygen
which seemed so lacking amid
the wallpaper and tapestries
rushes to fill his breathing.
Was the cab on its way? —
no matter — he would turn the corner,
away and out of her sight at last.

Gone was the death-urge that brought him here
to a rust-belt town that even rust
had abandoned, as if old broth
were a cure for his tumors, as if
the thing that gnawed him
would stop gnawing if *she* forgave him
the sin of their decades' severance.

The free air wants to fill him.
He breathes hard breaths, short,
    then longer. No, it is still there,
odds not good if they cut him open.
He will go back to the sand and the coral,
    the indifferent tide,
the long, slow sunsets.

He pauses once, before the turn
to the safe side-street, feels eyes
like spider tendrils on neck-nape.
She is there;
she has ascended to the attic,
watching,
      mouth mouthing incantations
of arachnid web-pull.

He will not turn; he will not look.
Thank God, he thinks, the mad
do not go forth. They stay at home,
tethered to memory and failure,
eyes fixed at last on blankness,
a pale face in a rhomboid window.

Uranium fuel rod being installed into a nuclear reactor.

URANIUM BOY

to Andrew

You have two names   two natures —

A bomb-factory centrifuge
spits out your isotopes:

U-238 — world-bound,
locked by your weight
to a dismal wedding,
a slow decay to lead

U-235 — your dangerous self,
prone to explode
if pressured, fond
of random emissions,
sun-defying eruptions.

as U-238[1]
> you'll have your diploma,
> a serious girlfriend
> who's drawn to inert elements,
> dull as a pail of spent bullets

as U-235
> you'll have me
> thunderstruck,
> knees weak
> from your beta-gamma
> > X-ray overflow,
> eager to share
> the small explosions
> that grace your visits.

Together we leapfrog electron shells,
an aureole of blue light
surrounding us,[2]
your fuel rod trembling
in my reactor core

---

[1] Uranium, the chemical element used to make atomic weapons, occurs in nature as two isotopes, U-238 and the far rarer U-235. The two isotopes are separated using a centrifuge. U-238 is radioactive but cannot be used for weapons. Because of its weight and density, U-238 is used for bullets. U-235, if enough of it is put into one small space, produces a chain reaction, yielding heat and radiation. Fuel rods of uranium are inserted into a reactor and as they approach one another, useful heat is produced for power generation. If a quantity of U-235 is squashed into one small space, a nuclear explosion occurs. All Uranium decays over tens of thousands of years and becomes lead.

[2] The eerie blue glow inside a nuclear reactor is called Cherenkov radiation.

HYLLUS AND THE CHARIOTEER

Anakreon, to Hyllus:
Last night I followed you, to the foot
of your street, to that Dionysian ruin
where men and youths commingle 'mid
broken columns and pedestals.
I saw you, "virgin" Hyllus
in quadruped surrender
to a popular chariot driver.

I watched and heard it all
from the anonymous shadows:
the brutal, pathetic beauty of it,
the animal moans,
the false starts,
the invoking of gods,
the simultaneous gasps,
the hurried redress of tunic and belt,
the counting out of three small coins,

I almost laughed at how, departing,
you brushed aside my friend Harmodius
with that most wonderful line:
"Only the hand that has held a whip
can ever hold mine!"

Small wonder that I have never possessed you,
slave as I am of scribbling,
more fond of vowels than hard-edged consonants,
my only rod the stylus. How strange
when beauty seeks not its merited worship,
leaving its pedestal for the dust,
kneeling for the promise of certain pain
and its negotiated, small price.

BURNT OFFERING

Anakreon, to Harmodius:
About that letter, the fervent one,
the one you hinted you'd sell when I die,
mocking its shaking autograph,
intimating the scandal —

I know your threat is false.
last night in my sleep I saw
your hands on a crumpled scroll,
the thrust toward a sputtering lamp,
the tiny screams as my words,
my awesome and unrepeatable vows,
my praise of your unworthy beauty,
collapsed and withered in a blue-green flame.

You brushed the ashes from your gentle arms —
they scattered, mingled with dust motes,
rode a moonbeam in a moment's leap
toward ghosthood, then dissipated.
Only one moth, before its suicide,
dipped in the ash and shared
one final taste of my missive.

No Phoenix rose, the earth
did not open to swallow you,
and your disdainful triumph
did not diminish the cosmos.

Yet he who burns love letters
offends the Gods.
You dare undo my holy madness
with your little hecatomb
of paraffin and oil?
They will come back to sting you,
my salamander syllables.

Try and love anyone now! Your sunken cheeks
and pale complexion will drive all away.
All will know you are pursued and haunted.
You will wish you had kept the living scroll
when you see how Love, an ash-faced Fury,
comes back from Acheron,
a broom hag to drive
your suitors off,

nightmare's bedmate, engendering
alarming sores and bruises,
leaving you spent and exhausted
as though a nest of incubi
used you for practice.

For me, loving is my badge of honor.
And as for your shame and embarrassment
at being the object of a great man's affection,
your little burnt offering does you no good:

I kept a copy.

HEPHAISTION AND ALEXANDER

Sleepless Hephaistion
is watching the dawn
steal gold from Alexander's hair —
the dozing god for whom a globe
gave way, high on a rock,
asleep, their tent a sail to catch
the suneast rising.

Soon horns will stir the troops
into another march. All eyes
will be on the Macedonian boy
for his commands. Nations
lay by their futile defense
topple their deities,
Persia and Babylon supine
as women eager for conquering,
Asia and the scented Chin of Flowers,
and many-templed India
waiting for his aegis in temple dance
of preordained surrender.

Empire may steal him again for a day,
a bride may blush at his summoning
to seal another chain to Macedon —
but night will bring him back
(so dreams Hephaistion,
his hand upon unarmoured breast,
his lips upon the unscarred neck,
his eyes awash in godgold curls)

Since jealous gods listen,
he cannot say "I love you"
to the earth's emperor.
All he can do is whisper
to his own inner listener:

He'll meld the world into a ball,
repeople it with Hellene rule,
journey it from Atlantean to Eastern Sea —
yet all he is
and owns are mine!

Empire enough,
this naked conqueror
my arms enfold to heartdrum pulse.
Reft of the joy of being god,
it is enough
to possess one.

TRIPTYCH: A PHILOSOPHY OF LOVE

Eros,
child no more:
you have grown ripe for the tasting mouth,
tender neck tongued to shoulder line,
breast taut and sloping downward,
firm, yet yielding to a lover's fingers.
Priapic awakenings
in peach flesh,
thrust-throb yearnings,
seed-pearls cometing outward.
I set my eyes upon you,
son of mischief, heart-thief,
in each statue-perfect moment —
ah, winged-foot *kouros*, do not move!

The sand, as you approach edgewater,
hieroglyphs your passing.
Clouds brood in their play-space,
proud-shouldered shrugging you,
but the azure emptiness between
wind tugs your wild-fringed forelocks.

Then, to the dread of all, you vanish,
a confident plunge into black surf's wall.
Far out, among the sharks and men-of-war
you give your loins to the waves,
foam-white with arm- and legstrokes.
When you turn back, the ebbing tide
tugs out and downward,
thrusts up green tentacles,
sea-crush craving
the hoarded air in your ribcage.

The place you sank from, eddying,
mocks me, longing's choke-thrust
suffocates — but there!

a lifeguard zephyr lifts you,
buoyant, defying wave and gravity,
your hair a boreal, golden banner
against the astonished horizon.

Why does every emptiness claim you?
Why are you always
one element removed from my longing —
legs run after wings in vain,
as talons for diving fish
or hounds for the tunneled hare.

Your name is no light thing.
I can scarcely say it, my hand
in greeting grasps too lightly
(fierce though, frail in action).
The place where your shoulder was,
my trembling hand, as though through water.

★★★

There never was an ocean.
We drank tea, in the city of Providence.
We listened to Mahler and Berlioz.
A closed door was always between our sleeping.
On Sunday, you fled the seven-hilled city.
I watched from my bench on the summit
as you hurtled down Angell Street.
Long I lingered, long I watched for you
as you turned down the twisted lanes.
And why do I most remember departures,
the back of you, your crossbow gaze
hurling its bolts on everyone but me?
Did our locked eyes frighten you?

One's young self delighting me,
one's older self, me, a dread to you?

Even the absence
of your image, an outline
I can trace in the air before me,
seems too beautiful to touch,
unbearable Phoebus, my searing star!

2

Philia,
more rare than lust, more lasting,
desiring all and yet beyond desire;
the unseen walker-beside of my dreaming,
first ear, first *thou* to my thoughts and writings,
comforter of solitudes,
the perfect other in silent communion.
For you the bread is baked, the teapot full,
the door ajar, the sleeping place secure.
If you came for a day, or forever,
it is the same to me — what's mine is yours.
At night, the room you sleep in breathes with me,
a circadian darkness webbed with moonlight.
I need not dream when my day is dreaming.

Scarce half a dozen times I've met you now,
soul mate, mad artist, and fellow outsider.
How many leagues we've walked together,
how many ancient stones deciphered! Worlds
turned within us as we riddled science;
with thought alone we toppled cathedrals,
lived in all ages and nations together,
counted as friends the seers, sages.
(These mingled streams, these parting rivers,
friendship true in a world with so little honor,
with brothers who choose us, and whom we choose.)

3
Agape,
rarest and last you come,
friend of all who do not trade in beauty's coinage,
love's vestal hope outliving the body.

Once it is shared there is no giver, taker.
O gift, I cannot take you back,
Salut à moi, I cannot refuse you.
You bind me still to all recipients,
   to one I loved who hurled himself
      cinder-block roped from a bridge-top,
   to the ones I loved who found Jesus
      and finding lost their souls,
   to the psychedelic-singed amnesiacs,
   to passion's walking skeletons,
   to the timid ones, backward-glancing
      across the unlived years.

You are the bird-sleep stillness preceding the dawn,
the astonished hush that follows the thunderclap:
the aura of all benevolent silences.

At the unvisited cell of hag and hermit
your manna falls like meteor dust,
a boon and blessing from the ever-burning stars.
For those who dare translate your enigmatic verse,
tribe, shade and totem, time and sorrow, slip away
as all who strive become ensoul'd in one great heart.

This is the love of gods and philosophers —
the self-reflecting eye of everything
regarding itself kaleidoscope,
the ever-renewing cosmos of music,
collision of line and curve, the whirl
of fractal nature at the event horizon.
You are the heart of alchemy, the Midas wand
tingeing whole hemispheres with autumn gold,
your arc and climax not flesh
but *Hypsos,* the moment Sublime.

4
Three-faced,
    triptych in unity,
some loves defy naming.

Which icon face is yours?
Eros, Philia, Agape?

Lust was too quickly slaked,
the vows of fellowship too soon betrayed.
The aspirant god
yearned toward the zenith,
a wingless Icarus.

And you, my momentary captive,
caught in my weave of words,
am I to be your lover,
    brother,
        fellow spirit?

Is your yearning for hair and bones?
For hearth and soul mate?
For winged companions to Olympus?

For my part, I do not know,
    cannot define
my troubled and troubling affections.

And as for you,
    Adonis, Atys, Adonai,
who knows what you mean
by being beautiful?

28-20-18/ 50-22-19

i
28-20-18
What use to tell you now —
the five poems I showed you,
objects, I said, inspired
by some hopeless passion —
that *your* mahogany eyes
provoked my orphaned odes?

I polished them
that you might see yourself,
transformed
in coat of myth
within their glassy hearts,

to no avail.

A strange gulf
has opened between us.
Over dinner, you say
"Perhaps when I get
to be your age..."
As though we were aliens:
my twenty-eight years
against your twenty.
I all but say it:
that you and I
should become a we,
that the five poems
could become a hundred,
that my biographers
would struggle
   to know the who and why of you.
But then I do not say it.

I sit at the table alone.
Full of my wine and food,
you go off in search
of adventure.

I will do likewise,
almost certainly,
but your soft voice
and ebon eyes
will not pass easily
from my desire.

I am still alone
at midnight.
Hands reached for me
but I did not let them touch me,
voices called,
but they were not yours.
Eyes beckoned,
but they had only the sad glaze
of desperation.

Somewhere in the Village
you are being wooed
by someone under twenty.
I take the last poem I meant
to dedicate to you.
I wrap it around
a meteor. I hurl
it with wish-thought
into the heavens.

Perhaps when you wake
   to find it
has cratered your lawn,
you might perceive
my praise of you etched
in nickel and quartz,
the glint of diamond —

perhaps you'll ask
your bedmate —
eighteen, was he? —
to read it to you.
If he knows how to read.

ii
50-22-19
Now I am fifty.
My art student visitor
rips off his clothes,
jumps into my lap.
"I like older men,"
    he says,

and proves it,
night after night,
despite the girlfriend.

She sends him out for milk —
    he dashes in,
shirt off, pants down
in one incredible motion.
"I have ten minutes,"
he says. A tender touch
brief as a hummingbird's kiss —
who am I to refuse it?

A Brown student,
all of nineteen,
curly black hair
and a drop-dead smile
sends me an e-mail:
Would you like to embark
on a kinky
father-son relationship?

So when he visits,
amazing, unbidden,
like manna or a comet,
he kneels before me.
"Give me orders,"
    he says.
Life is good.

THE LOFT ON FOURTEENTH STREET

> Doors painted bright,
> the tapestries stitched brilliantly,
> the singing hall, the dance pavilion —
> all ashes now, their incense gone,
> their light engulfed in night,
> their echoes muffled, silent.
> Bring the lute, I will sing.
> *Pao Chao*, c. 465 CE.

Am I the only one who sees it? Up there. That third floor loft,
all dark, the one whose windows gape wide
     through every season,
the one whose ghost-white curtains, now grayed by soot
     and tattered
by wind-flap, flutter like flags of abandonment, a place
like a village deserted before a certain onslaught,
bereft even of spider webs or sunning cats or plants.
I wonder why owls or bats or pigeons haven't gone in
to penetrate the darkened space inside, for that at least
would tell me something. Dark panes tipped in
     to a darker space
give only one answer: a nullity, that no one lives here.
Is that a light? One glow — a distant yellow bulb somewhere
way back, relentlessly dim and dull, night and day burning.
No matter how long I linger, I've never seen shadow
nor any illumined thing beam back or obscure its glow.
If only some hand, with a wrist and an arm below it
would show itself, reach out to pull the window shut at last!
But it goes on and on, like some tortured modernist art
(blank canvas, untouched piano keys, actors not acting)
the flutter-flash of curtain at wind's beck, the solitary
beam of a single bulb on a tall and shadeless pole lamp.

Am I the only one who knows him? That man. It is his loft.
We met in Central Park — yes, in the shrubbery! — we met
the day he first arrived in America. I was the first
to touch and welcome him, new-found from far-off China.
He spent his first American night on the floor with me.
Our bohemian mattress was next to the printing press.

I helped him read the street signs, pronounce the words
   he needed
to navigate the days until his funds caught up with him.
We made love until dawn; he slept against me as light shafts
broke day into the concrete canyons and made palaces
of derelict old cast-iron dry-good stores, the dust-mite sun
the same everywhere, bringing a special urgent magic.

We have mere dozens of words between us. His "How you are?"
would never cease to be his American-English greeting.
His raven hair intoxicated me, his eyes caught me
with a sense of unpredictable intelligence.
As the months passed, our friendship blossomed.
   He was my gateway
to the best of a world that is all but hidden to most.
What feasts we savored in Chinatown! *Chen ma po tofu!*
Sea slugs in casserole! Beijing Duck! Dragon and Phoenix!
The *pi-pa*, the *er-hu*, the bright world of Chinese music,
mad whirl of the Monkey King, the death and return to life
of the Butterfly Lovers; the long dark conspiracies
of eunuchs and emperors, flute girls and fierce concubines,
of Empress Wu, and Ci Xi, the last dread Dowager,
seen on the dim screens of Chinatown movie theaters,
even the awful kitsch of *The Red Detachment of Women.*
One day I played, to his astonishment, "The East Is Red,"
mock-improvised on my harpsichord. His Middle Kingdom
he gifted me, as I brought him to Beethoven, Mahler,
Handel and harpsichords, his East, my West in harmony.

(But we were never one, despite my always wishing it.)
Manhattan's day-long man-show and its nocturnal orgies
drew him into the world of "always-chasing, never-caught."

I moved to Providence, a secretive city, a place
where none of the newly-dead were *my* dead,
   a place where Poe
romanced forlorn, where gambrel or mansard concealed
genetic errors, the deeds of avarice, locked attics
whose cedar trunks had seen Canton and Goa and Senegal.
His phone calls stopped; he never visited. That distance rose
like an angry dragon between us. I had ceased to be,

a faraway Zip-code denizen, a toll-call outlaw.
I heard that his mother had visited, furious with him
for his myriad boyfriends. "I want you married!" she shrieked.
"You pick one. Stay with someone. I don't care if it's a man!"

Alone, I continued along my own Chinese journey.
Weekends I drifted through Chinatowns — tea houses, the cry
and clamor of the opera house enthralling me again —
White Snake, The Golden Brick, The Peony Pavilion! —
museums and galleries and auction houses teaching me
the glory of Chinese painting, the breathless awe I felt
regarding a single porcelain bowl emblazoned with
five peaches in full blush bloom over which, in perfect arcs,
five bats fluttered — perfect long life in perfect happiness.
The Monkey King, the lord of Chaos, now graced my mantel.
Kuan-Ti, the lordly general with his golden halberd
guarded my doorway; my wall aflame as Yuan pagodas
perched in impossible perspectives on dream-shrouded hills,
and one great Taoist dragon emerged from a yellow scroll.
This, my house, compounded of so many things *he* showed me.
I thought of him often. The gulf of not speaking became
an ocean. There would be no story to this, if this were all.

2

> Those I have known and loved my lifetime through —
> How many can I count ? One hand's fingers suffice!
> — *Po Chü-I*, circa 820 CE

Even though I am now an "older man," I'm never drawn
to older men. But here, a cultured gentleman, Chinese
and kindly, a devotee of the arts and the opera,
invited me for dinner and mischief (in one of those
vast beds no doubt constructed for the Forbidden City.)
Some instinct told me, *Go with this. Some things are meant to be.*

As I had only just resumed my old Manhattan haunts,
I thought much about old friends, the lightning jabs I'd suffered
while reading so many obits and epitaphs, too soon,
too young, too many, my whole vast web of acquaintances
shattered; thought, too, of the disconnects that the years impose

on early friendships. Each one of them seemed
    more precious now
as I began to make, and receive, what I came to call
"the annual endangered species phone call." Always
I thought, there's *one* I'll see again, that fickle, spoiled, bad,
obsessive and art-loving, music-besotted fellow.
We were not done with each other, and I had come ten times
more into his world since we had spoken last. Where was he?

He was there in the phone book, yet no one answered, ever.
His neatly-typed name was glued above the lobby mailbox.
Each time I passed there now, I entered and rang the doorbell.
Always that window was open, always that one dim light
in the far darkness, the curtains like a warlord's banner.
Where was his face, that glance of recognition, "How you are?"

The dinner was past, the rosewood bed explored in the dark
in various positions. My host and I sat talking,
and he asked me how I came to know so much of China,
its culture and literature, its ways and its secrets.
And so I spoke of my friend, of our seeing *Liang Shan Po
and Chiu Ying-Tai*, the gender-bending *Butterfly Lovers*,
of our long but often interrupted friendship, of how
I had been trying in vain to reach him for months. "Perhaps
his mother has died and he's gone off to Taipei. Perhaps
he's made the often-dreamt-of journey to the mainland —"
"What is his name?" my host asked, interrupting me. I spoke
his names — the English one he'd taken, and the Chinese one.
His face fell, "I knew him. He came here often. His friends, too.
Mad for music. Big stereo. He painted — or tried to."
He paused, lifted his cup of pale oolong. "Six months ago —
about six months ago, he died of AIDS."

                                                  The breath was ripped
from me. My heart sank; I felt I'd hurtle downward
to the earth's core if someone didn't catch me. "I'm sorry —"
he started, and then our eyes met and we realized it —
that we had met so he could tell me this — of all the men,
the myriad lonely American men he might have invited home.
The message had passed between us as a death-white cloud —
a thunder-blasted peach tree in a sky devoid of bats.

Later that night — how could I not? — I walked
    on Fourteenth Street.
The curtains still billowed, the panther eye-beam yellow light
still glowed. His name was still there — the rent still paid
    from afar
by his mother? — his things still up there uncollected?
    the paints,
those sketched-and-then-abandoned canvases piled up
    in a heap —
a great, dusty horde of art books and classical music —
or — nothing? a vast, dead space of which that shorn drapery
was but the fringe, a Mongolian waste of unslaked hunger,
a never-relenting sandstorm — and far, far off, a tomb
lined with the terra-cotta likenesses of his lovers?
(Which one was his death? To which of them was *he* Death?)
    No more!

3

    Oh, that I could make the world-globe shrink,
    so that suddenly I'd find you back at my side.
              —*Wang Chien (830 CE.)*

Art is the great denier when the artist is silent.
I waited all these years to write this, as though my silence
would cancel his passing, and the maelstrom that took him, too.
Perversely, I'd open a phone book and find his name there.
Why? I'd pass those windows, open, the curtains billowing.
Why? A whole year passed. One day the panes were pulled
    shut tightly.
There! A new name, neatly writ and pasted on the mailbox.
You see! He is dead! It is as final as a tombstone,
as final as the phone book, which no longer lists him now.
And more — it is as though he never existed. To me
alone was bountied that first night's touching,
    mine the laughter
of all the days we shared (that never a fraction of all
I was willing to give!) But still I had no tears for him.

Art is the great denier when the artist is silent.
Can world and time erase their errors? Another year passed.
I found myself on that block again. Windows were open!
Perhaps if I rang the doorbell, the new tenant would share
some shred of knowledge about the eccentric prior tenant —

I froze as I stood before the mailbox. The tenant's name,
that new, hand-lettered name had come unglued, it was
gone, fallen off, ripped off, or it had gone *pentimento*
(just as old paintings reveal some older art beneath them),
his name asserting itself, just as his absence ruled here.
I turned and fled, and I did not look up at those windows.

Imagine a tentative life, so lightly lived,
a dragonfly, an iridescent blur of wing, so light
that all that remains of him is his name, a mere undercoat,
a line on a page in a discarded old year's phone book,
a scratched-out entry in a hundred men's pleasure journals.

Three breaths, his real name on the wind (his name unspoken
except in my heart, and in the dream of autumn thunder) —
not in a tomb with white flags fluttering — not burning joss
at his ancestral shrine — but only, this moment, remembered.

STEVEN, TWENTY YEARS AFTER

To my open window from another open window
comes a night cry — a young man's cry as he gives himself up
to another man's urging, and they have both surrendered
to something greater, deeper, darker than they comprehend —
and I remember that cry so long ago as my own cry.

One August night in Manhattan's density I found him,
sometime between midnight and two in an abandoned place —
some warehouse or loft I can no longer place or name,
except it was near the river and many men lingered
there, and he was alone, the center of no one's favor,
auburn-haired, tall, bespectacled and out of place — as I
was, searching for love in the worst locales, as we all were,
questing for pearls in a pea-soup murk of mere touching.
We alone, we not drunk or drugged or desperate, we two
locked eyes and locked minds and stood
      against a wall entangled
one in the other's arms, and I said simply, "I want you."
He seemed astonished, uncertain, as I dragged him homeward,
to my loft where, in between the harpsichord and the press,
I simply and absolutely surrendered beneath him.

For some years we joined and parted, and in those years,
the joining was always unquestioned and automatic.
In a way I could not then define, *we fit together*.
Despite all this I never knew him — he was a poet
too, and conspired to hide from me all signs of his writing.
In my godless universe he kept his Catholic soul
safe from my sight. His English name had a secret as well,
concealing a famous Polish surname no one would fault.
He became a Quaker, finally, and his silences
became another layer of disguise and removal.
He never gave me the key of loving him, and when he
left for good he took all but a blood-red pitcher, that and
a Japanese bowl I still keep and always have with me.

And then the plague years came and claimed him
	and took him away
to Florida, whose warm clime, he told me, added four years
to his doomed span. I saw him on his visits to Manhattan —
he looked the same to me, unlike the walking skeletons
that drifted through the Village. I helped him publish a book,
a thin anthology of verse by reticent Quakers.
We met at Swensen's Ice Cream Parlor on 4th Street — at least
that's the last place I remember seeing him — until the call
from his brother: "I'm sorry to be the one to tell you
that Steven died last week in the hospice in Florida."
"Oh dear," I said, and mumbled something.
	The line went dead.
The brother didn't leave an address or number; perhaps
he didn't need or want to know why he was calling me,
why I was on the list of oh, so many names to call.

Strange how death numbs us. I have written much of longing
and almost nothing of having. I wrote no word of him
in all these twenty years, but in my sleep last night I dreamt
of another priapic August night, in Central Park,
how long past midnight, we two sought out a boulder-top,
and naked beneath the stars and a crescent moon, made love,
how we knew that many eyes were probably watching us —
lurkers and lovers and lunatics unloosed in the night —

and how a stately, tall black man stood over us suddenly,
and said, "I wonder if you young fellows need company.
My name is Hiram." He reached down.
	"Here's thirteen inches."
We laughed, told him how pleased we were to make
	his acquaintance,
but we were quite content with things as they were progressing.
"A rain check, then," the gentleman said, smiling, and vanished
to the discrete dark of the ever-watching shrubbery.

And so last night it all came back to me in a mind-flash —
his body against me, the soft blond hairs on his forearm
bleached white in starlight, the metamorphic rock
cool and hard beneath us, the eyes that watched, the scimitar
of moon above the museum ramparts, the long stillness
as we breathed in unison and wondered
    where our clothes were —
and as I thought of all this I cried out in the night,
a wild wail of grief and loss —
    gone to where, these twenty years?

Beyond what walls is love entombed in protestant silence?
How long, grief's pilgrimage, before the bitter coming-home?
Until the heart, on the soul's island, entire of itself,
tells the whole truth and holds back nothing, till solitude
rings out its *requiescat* and the secret of all touching
is finally revealed, this world of loving filaments
entwined with a common joy — a wild wail of grief and loss
escaping from me on this cold twelfth night of November.

SLEEPING WITH THOR

There might as well be a neon sign outside
that flashes "Vacancy," for all the talk I get from you.
Your great blond hulk beside me, breathing,
that one arm holding me, tight as a battle trophy:
all fine and good. Dane, or Viking, or as you joked
when you dragged me back here, "The great God Thor
in exile from Asgard," your open mouth is wordless,
as animal slumber, not quite a snore but a rumble
rolls over me. At the foot of the bed, your sandals,
somewhere safely off, that hammer named Mjolnir
that I think means more to you than boyfriends:
all fine. I should just relax and enjoy this, but for
the fact that you are sleeping with both eyes open
and I am staring into two tenantless holes where once
those commanding blue orbs had sundered my resistance.

Twice you have stirred, and wordless, twice
we have done everything you thought I wanted — god,
things I never even dreamt of! Even with all that armor on,
each touch was just at the cusp between joy and too much
to bear. If that was mead we drank, I'll toast the maker,
but must I go eyeless too into some zombie slumber?

Are you in Asgard, where Odin even now scolds you
for your college-boy dalliance? Remember to tell him
I am a poet, and a fit companion and confidant!
Your strong hand will not release me; clad
in the tatters of what you tore from me, I must wait
for the next installment, or canto, or conquest.

Are you in and out of yourself as it conveniences?
Those blue eyes drilled me, as you enjoyed the spoils
of my all too easy surrender. But what I win
is this manikin semblance of a lover,
the fox's calling card, a henhouse full of carnage
and a room chill-blasted with Arctic air.
(Good trick, since it is July outside.)

If you are phantom, a frosty incubus,
perhaps the rest of you will follow your errant eyes.
I will wake then, embracing a suit of armor,
a limp red cape and leggings.

I'll look down empty corridors of clothes, find no one
either up your sleeves or down your trousers, the shape
of your strong legs only an imprint on the mattress.
If I reach in those vacant sockets, I'd feel my fingers touch.
I'd know the embrace that holds me was death's rigor;
I'd feel for the cold hand inside the chain-mail glove:
try as I might for a pulse I'd find none. I'd dare
to place my lips to yours, expecting no respiration.

Dark raven wings flutter.
I think I hear a distant wind, a sigh between your ears
and mine. Perhaps it comes from Asgard, perhaps
you ride the Bifrost to return to me. Can I be bard
to your impossible beauty? Or when those eyes
assume their blueness, will the only words you mutter
be something about hockey practice, too much to drink,
and the need for a serious breakfast?

I expect nothing. I tell myself
I imagined most of this. But there,
the armored breastplate presses me still from behind,
and that arm refuses to release me,
and there, next to our hastily thrown off jackets,
reposes Mjolnir, the square-ended hammer of Thor.

DAN'S T-SHIRT

I've never wanted to be
an inanimate object
until now —

that T-shirt,
and the way it fits you,
one moment draped
like a chaste tunic
on an Attic statue,
the next revealing
each subtle curve
of shoulder, neck,
sinew and nipple —

how it possesses you
all the way down
from neck to pelvis,
how it knows your breathing,
your heartbeat,
the salt of your sweat.

I would be
that T-shirt.
Wear me for days
until I'm close
as a second skin.
Maybe you'll wear it
when you're with
your boyfriend.
Stains are good.

Then, when I stink,
I'll suffer the laundry,
the little hell
of the tumble dryer,

if I can take my place
in your dresser,
waiting my turn
as you slide into me,
head first, arm, arm,
the long slide down
your slender torso, ah!

And since I've shrunk
just ever so much,
being your T-shirt
just gets better and better.

THE PRICE

A thousand pearls I'd give
for the line of your neck and shoulders;
a Ming tomb's plunder
for the two-way sweep
of your raven hair;
a mountain of jade I'll yield
for the arc line
between your wrist and fingertips;
a bronze bell orchestra
with thirty attentive players
I'd trade for the symphony
of my name sung
in your soft tenor;
a thousand Bodhisattvas
for the two all-seeing orbs
beneath your lashes
(your third eye, mine already!);
all my Swiss bank accounts
for the curve of your back
pressed against me;
and for your thighs,
o take the world! take it!

EL PRECIO

¿Cuantas de perlas daría? Mil,
por la línea de su cuello a su hombro;
el pillaje de un sepulcro de Ming
por el doble movimiento
de sus cabellos de cuervo;
entregaría una montaña de jade
por el arco entre su muñeca
    y sus dedillos;
una orquesta de campanas de bronce
con treinta músicos atentos
cambiaría por la sinfonía
de mi nombre cantado
    para su voz tenor y dulce.
¿Cuantas de Bodhisatvas daría? Mil,
por los dos orbes que ven todo
    debajo de sus pestañas
(¡su ojo tercero, ya lo poseo!);
todo de mis cuentas de banco suizo
por la curva de su espalda
apretándome
y por sus musíos
¡o, tome la tierra! ¡Lo tome!

LOVE SPELLS

Disproof of ritual magic:
incense and candles, amulets and spells.
Try hard as you will, you cannot make
an oblivious boy love you. I know.
I have tried. Despite the aid
of an army of phantom helpers,
arrow-laden translucent Cupids,
satyrs ascending fire-escapes,
garden Priapi all compass-pointing
from his bedroom to mine;
in spite of love-arbors made
of djin-gathered roses
from the grave of Omar Khayyam;
in spite of the mandolin serenatas,
the gypsy fiddles, the er-hu, the lute,
the mournful barrage of hautbois
and Arcadian shepherd pipe,
he heard not a single chord
that brought my name to his lips.

Not even the darker spells availed:
despite the panic that seized
his would-be lovers
as bodiless wish forms stalked them
on empty street, scaling to the height
of penthouse with dacoit ease;
despite the solitude my magic cast
around him, still in that emptiness,
I was not the one he called to fill it.
The lovers fled; he fled their fleeing.

Vain the midnight oaths and promises
I made to dubious monarchs of love,
half-seen in the smog of my sulfurous hearth,
as I bartered to black-eyed Erys
(love's phantom in Pluto's domain),
a year of my life, for a night of his.

"Later," the hard bargainer said,
placing the coin back in my hand,
"Wait, and he will be with you always."
Now, with ashes and Styx between us
I know the full scope of the contract refused:
The coin is for the boatman.

SEE YOU

Ah, here's your friend Brett!—
    I look up at a familiar voice, two shadows
    upon me at outdoor café table
    two hands reach out
        long time no see   we all sing out.
They stand behind petunias' rail
    no move to join me   they have already lunched
    and are on their way to a concert
I regard my friend   as elegantly thin
    as ever   designer shades,
    an understated jade pendant
    concealing his delicate throat.
I remember our last visit,
    the spotlit red carpet
    in his cave-dark onyx bedroom,
    the many abandoned canvases
    of models who wouldn't be still
        or wouldn't return.
I ask, *How is your painting going?*
    the kind of query that,
        in my circle,
    weighs in a thousand times more
    than *How's your mother?* or
    Is the boyfriend still living there?
Ah, he says, *I can't paint any more.*
    I have . . . a handicap.
    His beautiful hands flutter
    in a remembered arc of brushstroke.
We talk of other things, and then,
    as they are leaving,
    I gave him my number.
See you, I called to their retreat,
    half-said, half-asked.
See you, he mumbled, hollowly.

I finished my meal, went on
    with my life. The years,
gods! decades I've slept between
those words and the thunderbolt
that stuns and befools me:
the way his friend, as they departed,
reached down and took his elbow
and steered him. He was blind.

PAST THE MILLENNIUM

SNEAKERS

for Dennis Barone

What do they signify,
   those sneaker pairs
   laced taut to their partners
      and hurled
   to hang in perfect balance
   from phone and power wires,
   fencetop of concertina wire,
   or from one skeletal tree
      selected alone of its brethren
      as a candelabra for old footwear?

Is this a bully-boy custom,
   first in a long
   chain of humiliations
   the weak must endure from the strong?
Yet I never see
   a shoeless boy whimpering,
   passing a bookbag gauntlet
   between rows of angry mountain bikes.
Each foot I see is Nike, Adidas
   New Balance or Reebok clad.
The children here are better shod
   than most armies.

Is it a rite of passage?
   do boys no-longer-virgin celebrate
   with new sneakers,
   flexing the old ones
      with base/basketball arms
   deftly over the waiting wire?
When, one mid-August morning,
   a half-dozen appear,
   dragging to droop the cable TV line,
does Lola, the knowing street's
most thoroughly bad girl, descend
   from her brownstone stoop, stand

under the newly-placed trophies, count
    one by one, click-tonguing
Jose, Luis, the other Jose, then Eddie,
Enrique, then Juan — no,
it was Juan, then Enrique ...

Or is it magic, the outgrown
    tooth fairy gone fetish,
retrieving those perfectly good pairs
of perfectly matched sneakers
from dumpsters and garbage bags
    and placing them,
for those who dare a fall
    or electrocution,
like elf-gold or foxfire —
who so foolish as to climb there
    to claim the treasure,
to risk a fairy-snatching
    at arm-reach distance?
Do they in turn
    upon being transported
    leave only *their* shoes behind?

What do they signify?
I dread to ask the boys who throw them.
They are the same boys, born and reborn
    who mocked me in the schoolyard
for carrying books like a girl —
    for reading books at all
        in the summer —
as hawk to hare, they would know me.
Perhaps the crow on the wire,
    the raven on the chosen tree,
the ledge pigeon
will tell me.

OLD POET GLIMPSED ON THE SUBWAY

At 5 p.m. on a Monday night
on a subway car at Wall Street,
amid the pack and crush of crowds
I glimpsed once more the old poet,

one arm bent round upon itself.
A stroke had crippled him —
The great light of his eyes
    had gone out.
There was no more panther in him,
and the shrill gulls
    had taken his words.

He had always been
more prey than poet:
hard boys would follow him
home from the bank each payday.
His superiors marked him
as a man they need not advance,
a reliable cipher,
the kind who die at their desks.
They knew nothing of his poetry.

Not seeing me, not seeing
anyone, he did not look up
from his morning reading
(if mumbling the price of mutual funds
    can be called reading).
Perhaps he dreaded the gaze
of the latest predatory mugger,
or worse, the accusing eye
of a poet who remembered him.

I left the car. It hurtled on.
I only saw him that one time.
I had published his first,
    and only, book.

THE TWENTIETH CENTURY

We thought the world would end.
We thought the world would end.
    It didn't end.
        We ended.

TNT uranium   hydrogen neutron
cobalt strontium   mushroom clouds —
those megatons   were mega-nothings.
Our sleepless nights the averted nightmares
of Holocaust and zombie aftermath.
Shelters and radiation suits,
clickety-click-click of Geiger doom,
roaches inheriting our empty cities.
These didn't happen. But the earth's doom
sits in missile-tip submarines,
ever flying bombers, subterranean launch holes
to the delight and profit of various cartels

But we began to die anyway.
The least minds of our generation
adrift in the poppy-coke ecstasy-grass
hallucinogenocide snort-shoot-smoke death derby
to the delight and profit of various cartels
or we stumbled sleepless
in shopping mall airport Times Square
shilling Bibles or Vedas or Mormon blather,
getting clear with Scientology,
drinking the Kool Aid in Jonestown,
or calling the fat old Korean
munitions maker the honest to God Jesus Two
to the delight and profit of various cartels

or we loved one another to death,
became pestilent walking skeletons
in our holy orgy cities
New York and San Francisco,
and the dregs of medicine

experimented upon the poor
to the delight and profit of various cartels

We thought the world would end.
We thought the world would end.
      It didn't end.
           We ended.

SOLZHENITSYN IN NEW YORK

A spectre is haunting
the orchestra.
Bolshoi Opera
at Lincoln Center
on its New York visit;
exile in his seat,
down from his Vermont
dacha for a slice of
Mussorgsky's Old Russia.

Onstage, the false Dmitri,
a mad young monk
who believes himself
the murdered Tsarevich
restored by miracle to life,
approaches his destiny —

the guilty Tsar clock-shrieks
the impossibility
of the boy he already killed
an impossible boy
whose rebel army advances
now upon the Kremlin.

How can such things be?
The dead must be commanded
to stay that way! A former person
cannot become a person again!
We have erased his name
from the history books!

Each throb of pendulum
heart-hammers him:
I killed you I'm coming
I saw you dead — An old man
saw me risen. The Poles
have already acknowledged me.

Usurper, imposter, ghost!
What use are borders,
what consolation exile
when they *come back*?

At break of act
the singers —
the dark-eyed Boris,
the blond Dmitri,
the hermit monk Pimen,
the Polish seductress,
scan darkened aisles
for one glimpse
of Alexandr Isaievich
whose name
    they are not allowed to utter
whose books
    they are not allowed to read

the novelist
a bristling field of names
a nation émigré in one,
a walking catalog
of uncountable deaths
on steppe and taiga.

You're dead,
the Kremlin telegrams.
I'm here, the exile
reminds his enemies.
One day I'll be *there*.
The held-in-check
will be checkmate.

Later Mussorgsky's
tyrant dies,
invoking god,
anointing a child tsar
to follow him:

I am still Tsar!
Ya Tsar yeshcho!
Boris falls dead
as tyrants must.
A truth-cloud waits.
It has all time to attend
to its business.
It will not let them sleep.

THE LINDEN TREE IN PRAGUE

*for Jan Palach, Czech martyr,
who set himself on fire January 16, 1969
to protest the occupation of his country*

1
Linden in Prague's Museum Square:
I was born, I was sown
of mother and father trees in some forest.
I screamed as the sun troped me out of the earth,
grew slowly in the shadows of tall buildings.
thrust out my blossoms at the hope of spring,
Years passed; I grew protective rings
around me. Exhorted into summer by sun
and the bacchanal of squirrels, I owe each year
millions of leaf-deaths and resurrections.
The solemn students and professors
stride by with dour looks, eyes locked
into the mysteries of Marx and Engels.

I must pretend to stand up straight.
I must not follow the mocking sun
    and its false revolutions.
I must wait for the ultimate paradise,
world's daylight redistributed for all.
I tremble as angry gardeners trim
the arrogant beard-branchlets
that fringe my still-adolescent trunk.
I am all passion and impracticality.
My heart-shaped leaves are on my sleeves
as I greedily drink sunlight, give shade
to those below in blossom-fall, exude the scent
that maddens lovers to *Unter der Linde* mania,
then paint myself in hues of gold and brown,
shedding my currency in one great shrug
as summer ebbs to frost-dawn.

Behaving well, it seems,
is not in my nature, despite those lectures
on dialectics I hear each afternoon
from the open lecture hall's window.

Much passes beneath my shadow:
across the square, crowds press
to bourgeois marriages and funerals —
the upright grooms go in,
the silver-handled caskets come out,
the church, the state, the people
move on in soot and sorrow, day to day.
On one side, Marx and Engels;
on the other, tradition, and just beyond
my line of sight that monument to Huss,
the great religious martyr. Conflict
divides us like the great Moldau.

We have lived through Kings and Empires,
bad governments and good. Everyone seemed
to think it was getting better last year.
But something has changed now:
Why do these people whisper always?
Why do so many avert their eyes from me?
Why does neighbor spy on his neighbor,
reporting every oddity to the men in black?
Why do I hear the rumble of thunder?
Why does the symphony break off
in the middle of rehearsing Smetana?
Why have the women gone to the cellars?
The earth shakes. Soldiers and tanks everywhere!
The streets are full of Russians and Poles,
Hungarians, Bulgarians, East Germans —
all of East Europe has come to crush us!
Men with fur hats speak swollen, Slavic words.
Death is here. The smell of blood is here.
My roots touch the entrails of the hastily buried.

Anger is everywhere. I hold my leaves,
make camouflage for lovers, conspirators.
Students rip down the street signs
and hide them in my upper boughs —
    the invaders drive in circles
      and cannot find their destinations.
I open my bark for secret messages,
encourage pigeons to carry the word
of where is safe, and who is betrayed.
I guess I am guilty of anti-people
tendencies — who would have thought?

Here comes that student, Jan Palach,
he's all of twenty-one, dark-haired,
a delicate face meant for poetry,
though worn by the study
of too much philosophy, too young.
He is the ardent one, the solitary dreamer.
And more: he intends to *do something*.
He and some others have made a vow,
a terrible pact. He will go first.
He is not Jan Huss,
    burned by his fellow citizens
        over the flavor of God:
he is just Jan Palach from Všetaty,
and he will burn in the world's eyes
because of Philosophy
    (Plato's tanks crushed
        the Age of Reason).

I am his un-indicted ally.
The winter ground is covered still
with the dried leaves of my autumn,
some damp, some dry and worn
    to little more than vein lines.
He scoops them up; he stuffs his coat with them,
fills his cap, book bag and pockets,
fuel and kindling for his mission.
He is the icon of our unhappiness:
he will open like a triptych of gold

into a flame to embarrass the sun.
He opens the can of gasoline,
and before anyone can stop him,
he explodes into a fireball,
a flaring marionette; he whirls three times
then falls into a curled ball
of incendiary horror.

2

Earth gives him no resting place.
    As mourners gather
in ominous groupings,
the men in black dig Palach up,
cremate his already-half-cremated frame
and send the urn off to his mother.
There, in Všetaty, no one is allowed
to give him another burial.
No graveyard dares take the ashes
    for half a decade.

In Prague, Palach's first grave
is repossessed. The state deposits there
the corpse of a nameless old woman.
On your way now, nothing to see —
just some old cleaning lady's grave.
No martyrs in this cemetery —
I'll see your papers please.

3
Twenty years on, a crowd will gather
for something called "Jan Palach Week,"
a pretext to take to the streets again,
and one day later,
    the Communist government falls.

Your ashes, Jan Palach, will return to Prague.
I will be beyond returning, for long ago
an angry axe man removed all trees,
to the despair of poets and squirrels,
the better to conduct surveillance
of all the law-abiding citizens.

There, on the spot of his immolation,
a bronze marker, half cross,
    both Catholic and Slav,
lifts out of mosaic'd pavement.
My last root is hidden beneath it,
as leaf by dry leaf, and ash by ash,
my ghost is a receptacle for tears, and memory.
I was there, around and within him.
I, too, exploded for Liberty.

— October 1969, New York, revised 1986,
rewritten 1996; rewritten 2011

SARAJEVO DOLLHOUSE

"All over the city sheets of burned paper, fragile pages of gray ashes, floated down like a dirty black snow. Catching a page you could feel its heat, and for a moment read a fragment of text in a strange kind of black and gray negative, until, as the heat dissipated, the page melted to dust in your hand." — (Dr. Kemal Bakarsic, librarian of Bosnia's National Museum, describing the burning of the National and University Library, 25-27 August 1992).

Let's play. It's Sarajevo 1992.[1]
A nice old European city.
Here's a doll house, a fine
old building near the urban center.
Artists and musicians live here,
to be near the concert hall,
the Conservatoire, the theaters.

But something has gone amiss.
The front wall,
which we, as gods,
were accustomed to opening
so we could examine our dolls,
is gone, blown to a thousand
shards and smoldering cinders.

Amid the tumbled chimneys,
the shattered slate of rooftops,
a broken piano lies upside down
and cannot right itself.

---

[1] Beginning in April 1992, Serbian nationalist attacks on Bosnian cities and towns deliberately and successfully targeted national libraries, museums and archives, in the process wiping out nearly the entire written record of Bosnia's history.
Among the losses is Bosnia's National Library in Sarajevo, which also contained the university's holdings and the country's national archive of newspapers and periodicals. Prior to its destruction, the National Library held over 1.5 million volumes, including 155,000 manuscripts and rare books. It was bombarded for three days with incendiary grenades on August 25-27, 1992, and was reduced to ashes.

A French horn has melted,
into a grandfather clock,
its twisted face now telling
not time, but terminus.
A writer's desk has leaped
onto an awning, loose
sheets of an interrupted epic
up and out on the wayward breeze —
the doll pages are tiny as postage stamps
and in their updraft they meet
the downward fall of burning paper,
ash glowing on text as the letters
burn hotter than the space
that framed them.

Why did the dolls not run away
when the nearby library exploded?
The exposed rooms tell all:
how the dreamers, the writers,
the mad ones with all the operas in them
refused to leave despite the danger.
"No one — not even a Serbian —
would bomb the library, right next door."
A grandmother doll,
white-haired in her rocking chair,
teacup and silver platter beside her,
listens to Bartók on tiny headphones —
listens forever, and her eyes are gone.

The room above, the garret
where we left the hungry poets
to their own devices last time —
(Rodolfo and Mimi from *La Boheme?*)—
is still a wild tangle of lovers' limbs.
but they are all asunder —
two heads locked in a melted kiss,
pairs of legs and arms
under the sheets at impossible angles,
a single foot cut off at the ankle,
four shoes at the door, going nowhere.

The gaunt violinist who looks
ever so much like Paganini,
sits in his underwear rehearsing —
fiddle to chin and left hand
fingering a great arpeggio —
the arm with the bow
is nowhere to be found.
The dramatist is in the other garret.
His fountain pen is raised, his eyes
look up in astonishment — words cannot say —
his legs have run off without him.
Mock crows pick at his leg bones,
amid the branches of the mock plane tree.

Our doll house has fared better
than those of our neighbors.
The dolls' University is a shambles,
some pyromaniac child
burnt up the libraries — just walls
remain, an outer shell
surrounding an ash pit.
The acrid smell of burnt
plastic fills the air —
toy soldiers consumed,
along with toy firemen,
nurses and local police.
There's even a Mosque
with a burnt-up little Imam
and little singed prayer carpets.

But all is not lost.
We manage to gather
a dollhouse orchestra
and send it to play
in the library ruins.

We thank our stars
that none of this happened
in the larger world,
that the child with matches
has been punished,

that the melted, shattered
denizens of our house
can be replaced

with new ones.
No harm done.
No one would bomb
a library,
a museum,
a concert hall!

AUGUST RECESS

Reform, like
    Zeno's arrow,
            never comes:
before the halfway measure
must come the quarter measure,
before it
the hemi-demi-semi measure,
before it the intention,
never mind the will.
Lacking the single push of empathy
the bowstring is unreleased because
it was never pulled.
The fat hand, weighted
with golden rings,
the leaden-braceleted
wrist, the immobile arm
en-Midas'd by bribery.
Fear no arrows from this
sclerotic Congress.

OCTOBER THOUGHTS IN WAR TIME

What does October mean?
   To the old Bolshevik the month we finally took
      what was ours —
   to the old émigré the month we lost everything,
   and had to flee to the border.
To the Spanish and Portuguese, Italians and Greeks,
taking café in treeless plazas,
the aftermath of equinox, a few brown slurries of oak leaves
skittering from Alps to the sea, not a time, but a passing,

To the Chinese, a mottled dream of maple, gingko,
ailanthus and willow, in which one pale
and angular scholar, his beard as thin as an artist's brush,
takes tea in his gazebo, as the autumn's white tiger
runs down the bounding deer.

For me, in this New England city,
it is not quite autumn.
I spy the moon's new crisped crescent
hovering above the Hopkins house.
An angry Mars is at its nearest —
all these heavenly bodies tugging at treetops.

The Unitarian bell tolls eight, as Uranus,
a dim flickering, grazes the steeple
as though curious to know
for whom the clabber sounds the bronze.

The weary earth has had enough explosions.
Winter will yield up autumn,
if autumn will erase its merry carnage.
If leaves do not fall, perhaps the heads of state
will leave decisions   undecided,
prisoners un-decapitated,
toxins unmanufactured,
uranium un-enriched —

perhaps the deadly elements
will go unmined, the gray bombers
unmanufactured,

the hateful thought, snug in its walnut,
from its high branch
unfalling.

PRESIDENTIAL UPDATE

Deaths down in Iraq! Yes, really!
Only a thousand killed this month!
This is progress.
Four hundred thousand weapons
have gone missing, admittedly,
but as the NRA can tell you,
guns don't kill people,
people kill people.
Last month we obviously succeeded
in killing the people
who killed everyone the month before.
Now that's a good policy:
kill everyone who kills anyone,
except, of course, us.
Next question, please —
    not you, not you,
    not you, not *you* —

THEOLOGY 101

My proof
  that religion
    is unnatural:

if you put a bishop's hat on a dog,
  it will do everything
  within its power
    to remove it.

While it wears the hat,
  no other dog
    will have anything
      to do with it.

THE BLACK HUNTSMAN

(after Victor Hugo's *Le Chasseur Noir*)

"Who goes there? You, passer-by,
why choose these somber woods,
vast crowds of crows a-flutter —
no place to be with a rainstorm coming!"
"Make way! I am the one
who moves in shadow.
Make way! — for the Black Huntsman!"
The leaves on the trees,
    which the wind has stirred,
are whistling, and I have heard
that all this forest
    will be a-shiver with shrieks
when the storm-cloud clears
and the moon shines down
on the Witches' Sabbath!
Why tarry here? Go chase the doe,
run down the fallow deer,
out of the forest to the unplowed fields.
And more than deer: this is your night
to bag a Tsar, or at least,
an archduke of Austria,
    O Black Huntsman!

The leaves on the trees —
    Hasten, Black Huntsman,
    to sound your horn-call,
    fasten your leggings
    for a long ride.
    The easy stag who comes grazing
    in plain sight by the manor?
    Ah, no, ride down the King,
    ride down a Bishop or two,
        Black Huntsman!

The leaves on the trees —
    It rains, the thunder
    roars, the flood
    sends rivers raging.
    Refuge engulfed, the fox
    flees this way, that way,
    no shelter anywhere, no hope!
    Take not the easy prey:
    there goes a spy on horseback,
    there a judge in his carriage —
        take *them*, Black Huntsman!

The leaves on the trees —
    Do not be moved
    by those monastic flutterings
    in the wild oat-fields,
    those spasms of St. Anthony's
        Satanic possession.
    Hunt down the abbot,
    spare not the monk,
        O Black Huntsman!

The leaves on the trees—
    Your hounds are on the scent.
    Go for the bears;
    leave no wild boar unslaughtered.
    And while you're at it,
    doing what you do so well,
    Black Huntsman,
    hunt down the Pope, the Emperor!

The leaves on the trees —
    The wily wolves side-step you,
    so loose the pack upon them.
    A stream! The track is lost
    in a teeming waterfall.

But what is this? An ex-president
    without his secret service men!
    And there in that cave,
    a former vice-president cowering!
    Run, hounds! Bring them to ground!
        Well done, O Black Huntsman!

The leaves on the trees,
    which the wind has stirred
    are falling, and I have heard
    that the dark Sabbath
    with all its raucous shrieks
    has fled the forest.
    The cloud is pierced
    by the cock's bright crow:
    the dawn is here!

All things regain their original force.
My nation becomes herself again,
    so beautiful to behold,
a white archangel robed in light,
    even to you, Black Huntsman!

The leaves on the trees,
    which the wind has stirred
    are falling, and I have heard
    that the dark Sabbath
    with all its raucous shrieks
    has fled the forest.
    The cloud is pierced
    by the cock's bright crow:
    the dawn is here!

From Victor Hugo's *Chatiments: "Le Chasseur Noir"*

VETERANS' DAY PARADE

The peg-legged cats of New Bedford
march with the handicapped mice,
Half-worms and headless mantises,
ransomed from the mouths of robins,
barely keep up with the centipede marshal,
twenty-seven legs shy of a hundred.

One-winged bats fly tandem,
an air show of squeaking somersaults.
Singed moths and poisoned dragonflies
careen and smoke like wounded biplanes,
sky-writing dyslexically
the place-names of recent battles.
A buzz-huzzah rises from the float
of wingless flies (playthings
of wayward boys or of a vicious god).

There is a war on, but still
the parade stumps and staggers
to amputee drumbeats
and fingerless fluting,
one-lung horn calls
snaggle-tooth riffs
abruptly voiced and just
as abruptly silenced.
Foot, feeler, stump and tentacle,
cane, stick and crutch
time-tap the slow march,
the Dead March, the *Marche Militaire*,
wave after wave of the wounded,
proud of their medals.

The blind bishop, a miter'd mole,
waits at the bandstand.
Though deaf, he will bless on cue,
to cornets and drum rolls,
as the gulls, in chorus, incontinent,
take aim at the generals' helmets.

Wheelchairs and walkers snap in salute
as the bishop raises,
    on the end of his hand-hook, the trans-
substantiated Host
assuring them all of eventual reunion,
    (after the Victory)
with their missing body parts.

THE PROPHET BIRD

I have heard the shrill call of your prophet bird.
Night and the moon have brought me out
to the sea shore to hear its funereal song.
I will not weep; I cannot despair.

I stand on this storm-blown, sea-rising
drought-ridden planet, yet my heart
does not sink, even as maniacs
wild-eyed and waving Kalashnikovs & holy-books
explode themselves and bring carnage around them,
even as I consider Europe a vast boneyard,
the Middle East a trash-heap of uncivilizations
    piled high since the first silt of Nile & Tigris
    gave idle kings & priests the criminal idea
that they, or their supernatural betters,
had dominion over everything, and for all time.
What creatures! Fashion a stylus or a horn of brass,
and then a scimitar. Invent polyphony,
then make for Torquemada
an exquisite device for torture's pain-song.
Should such vile animals,
    with the table manners of Harpies,
be written off by the Animal Kingdom,
turned out to thorn and briar by the Plants,
poisoned to extinction by acrid Minerals,
blotted by the very sun and stars?

I answer only that Beauty redeems everything.
Even the tiger, when it is not hungry,
    looks on the bounding gazelle
    as a thing of wonder.
For the line of one neck and shoulder
    on a Phidean marble,
one phrase of Handel or Mozart,
one heart-stopping dab of paint on canvas,
we are forgiven much. We share with life,
    from pseudopod to mammoth,
    from the most delicate tendril

  to the great bulk of whale-flesh,
the way the all-too-familiar disk
  of the sun-faced daisy might see us,
the fascinated horror we feel
  as we regard the the self-
   illuminating eye of the giant squid —
all monstrous to all, all beautiful to all

as long as life goes drunk on self-delight
  and aches for the touch of its kind,
as long as we know that all life enjoys
  the benediction of earth-turn and sunrise
that the first word the Universe uttered
  was *Surprise!*

Another human chapter is ending.
It is not the end of everything
  (only the thin-lipped prophets
  with their dry-leaf Bibles
  believe that everything will end).
The story is not over.
It will never be over.
Walls and guard towers have fallen,
  death camps and prison camps closed.
All this is good. That some mass murderers
  sleep in their pensioned beds disturbs me.
That new Lenins and Berias and Stalins
  are waiting to be born, disturbs me.
But life itself has something in store for us.
We will star-leap if we must to another Earth
if we cannot learn from this one.
The air, yes, is a different color now.
Trees on the mountaintops brown in its acid.
If elm, beech and chestnut
  possessed a smiting god to call upon
the green world would rise and smother us:
but they do not as though even the earth's
last barren acorn can forgive us.

Full half of the cause of the harm we do
    is that we live so briefly,
so little time for giving and healing
    after so much seizing and taking.
So let us live longer, not less,
    let us become old-timers, undying,
        cyborgs if we must —
if all the great men and women past were there for us,
    even if only as their brains afloat in a tank
still they would come to us
    the way the ghost-Athena seized
        the sword-hand of Achilleus,
            saying to him, *Don't do that*

It is because we die
    that we make Earth an ashtray,
        choke ocean with petrol and stryofoam.

I do not worry much about banks, and mortgages.
Things fall apart, and pass away.
Their place will be taken by other things.
I would welcome the end of six-lane highways,
the tic-tac-toe of airplanes across the sky.
I see a different millennium unfolding
    not of steel girders and oil derricks.
So long as we escape the total madness
    of mouth-foaming God-told-me-so
        hand-on-Apocalypse men,
so long as our better natures prevail

I will live to see every book ever written
available free to everyone on earth,
Beethoven free, Homer and Virgil and Dante,
Shelley and Poe and Whitman for everyone,
a never-closing museum that all may walk
alone or in the best of company —

Your prophet bird
   would sing disaster,
minor in downward scale —
my bird, the melody inverts,
   beaking the flats away,
   my scale ascending.

ARS POETICA

WITH POE, ON MORTON STREET PIER

Sunset at the Manhattan piers: gray-black,
the iron-cloaked sky splays vortices of red
into the Hudson's unreflecting flow.
Blown west and out by a colorless breeze,
the candle of life falls guttering down
into a carmine fringe above oil tanks,
a warehoused cloud of umber afterglow,
hugging the scabrous shore of New Jersey,
a greedy smoker enveloped in soot.

To think that Poe and his consumptive Muse
stood here in April, Eighteen Forty-Four,
his hopes not dashed by a rainy Sunday —
an editor thrice, undone, now derelict,
author of some six and sixty stories,
his fortune four dollars and fifty cents.
Did he envision his ruin, and ours?
Did his eureka-seeking consciousness
see rotted piers, blackened with creosote?
Did rain and wind wash clean the Hudson's face,
or was it already an eel-clogged flux
when he came down the shuddering gangplank?

Who greeted him? This feral, arched-back cat,
fish-bone and rat-tail lord of the landing?
Did he foresee the leather'd lonely wraiths
who'd come to the abandoned wharf one day
in a clank-chain unconscious parody
of drugged and dungeon-doomed Fortunato
and his captor and master Montresor?

He gazed through rain and mist at steeple tops,
warehouse and shop and rooming house — to him
our blackened brickwork was El Dorado.
He needed only his ink to conquer
the world of Broadway with his raven quills —
Gotham would pay him, and handsomely, too!

Did the lapping waters deceive him thus —
did no blast of thunder peal to warn him
that this was a place of rot and rancor?

The city shrugs at the absolute tide.
I am here with all my poems. I, too,
have only four dollars and fifty cents
until tomorrow's tedium pays me
brass coins for passionless hours of typing.
I am entranced as the toxic river
creeps up the concrete quay, inviting me,
a brackish editor hungry for verse,
an opiate and an end to breathing.

Beneath the silted piles, the striped bass spawn,
welfare fish in their unlit tenements.
A burst of neon comes on behind me,
blinks on the gray hull of an anchored ship —
green to red to blue light, flashback of fire
from window glaze, blinking a palindrome
into this teeming, illiterate Styx.

The Empire State spire, clean as a snowcap
thrusts up its self-illuminated glory;
southward, there's Liberty, pistachio
and paranoid in her sleepless sunbeams,
interrogated nightly, not confessing.
It is not too dark to spy one sailboat,
passing swiftly, lampless, veering westward;
one black-winged gull descending to water,
immersing its quills in the neon mirror.

Now it *is* dark. Now every shadow here
must warily watch for other shadows
(some come to touch, to be touched, but others —)
I stay until the sea chill shrivels me,
past the endurance of parting lovers,
beyond the feral patience of the cat,
until all life on legs has crept away.

Still, I am not alone. The heavy books
I clasp together, mine and Edgar Poe's,
form a dissoluble bond between us.
Poe stood here and made a sunset midnight.
Poe cast his raven eyes into this flow
and uttered rhymes and oaths and promises.
One night, the river spurned his suicide.
One night, the river was black with tresses,
red with heart's blood, pearled with Virginia's eyes,
taking her under, casting him ashore.
One night, he heard an ululating sob
as the river whispered the secret name
by which its forgetful god shall know him,
his name in glory on the earth's last day.

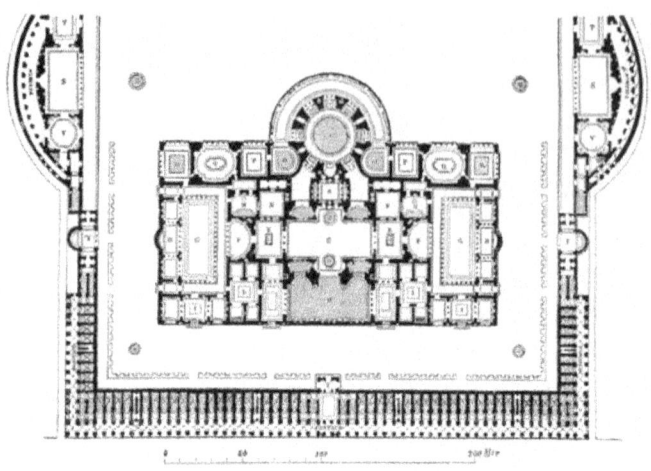

The Baths of Caracalla were built over the site of Numa's palace.

THE GARDEN OF NUMA POMPILIUS

> *simulat sibi cum dea Egeria congressus nocturnus esse*[1]
> — Titus Livy, *Ab Urbe Condita*, i. 9

From whom does the great king
gain his wisdom, the king
whose great laws pour
as from a river?
Some say a woman advises him,
but the king's house
has neither woman nor woman-child:
no dainty foot has walked here
since the consort's burial.

Some say, in his grief
    he has gone Orphic-mad,
and now a boy inspires him.
It's true that beardless youths
come freely, serving from silver
bowls and chalices. (Greek ways
and wiles — are they among us?)

---
[1] He himself pretended to be in nocturnal congress with the goddess Egeria.
— Livy, *History of Early Rome*.

<182>

This too is idle gossip —
for neither youth nor maiden
has seen the silent garden
of Numa Pompilius.
The summer's short nights
he sleeps alone here.
Scribes come at dawn
to take his judgments,
hear the new laws.
His wisdom astonishes,
surpassing, surprising
his ever-contending counselors.

The source of his power is here,
a stone-cut spring, old as the Tiber,
that only kings may drink from,
in the grave-scent of yew trees,
the bitterness of laurel —
a still voice that thrills him,
pale arms that come
from out of nowhere
to rest on his shoulders —
the voice above faction,
calumny, and conspiracy.

Rome is Numa, and Numa, Rome.
His, the rites to Jupiter,
the incense rising, entrails read;
his Virgins at Vesta's hearthside;
his, the temples of Mars and Janus,
the ordered calendar and the names of days —
his thoughts no sooner spoken than enacted.

Her thoughts. Those garden nights
he dare not look backward
to search her countenance —
madness or blindness
the nympholept's punishment.

She might be crone, or eyeless,
or Gorgon-locked, or nothing more
than poplar leaves rustling.
Her name on his lips,
an Etruscan mystery,
is all he has, or knows.

She will not have a temple,
chooses her own altar and pontifex.
He comes to the spring font,
to the branches bowed
with night-wind,
calls thrice (their only ritual) —
Egeria! Egeria! Egeria!

EPIGRAMS

Always check pigsties for pearls:
many have fallen in.

    ★ ★ ★

Two in the bush
is the root of all evil.

    ★ ★ ★

If you go to a place,
and you find it is Sparta,
then you must make it Athens.

DANNY AND BEATRICE

I — Personals Ad Postings

3/14 — Mystery Girl at the Fountain   M4W — 9
Today, at De Pasquale Square, at the fountain.
You in a red top, blond.
I like you better than Madonna.
Was that your mom or your sister with you?
She gave me a dirty look (how I wanted
to come up and speak to you!) I didn't mean
to stare. When I saw you, Time stopped.
The Bells at St. Joseph's Church, right then,
that instant, they started ringing two.
I know because my watch stopped:
it was 1:59 exactly. So if you see this,
I just want to be friends, OK?
I'm in the third grade at St. Boniface.
You're maybe my age.
Next week at the fountain? LOL

Re: Mystery Girl at the Fountain   M4W — 35
Who do you think you're kidding?
You're just some nasty pedophile.
Stalking that little girl, are you?
How old are you, 40? I'll bet you're on
that sex offenders list. Or you're one
of them child-molesting priests!
I'LL TRACE YOU AND I'LL CALL THE FBI!

Re: Mystery Girl at the Fountain   M4W — 9
Hey people! I posted the message. Attached
you'll see my picture. Not some old dude, see!
And I'm nothing like Father Francis,
the priest they took away for pinching and rubbing.
I just wanna meet her. She's not like anyone,
not like anyone on the whole planet.
The sun stopped when she looked at me.
I'm not dangerous. I plan to be a poet.
I don't know why, but I think she can help me.

Re: Mystery Girl at the Fountain   M4W — 35
Nice try, pervert! I seen that kid's face before.
It's on a milk carton. Missing and exploited.
Leave the girl alone and get off Craigslist!

Re: Mystery Girl at the Fountain   M4W — 28
Cool off, everyone! I was at the fountain Saturday, too.
I saw how the boy stared at the little blond girl.
I even know the girl and her mother.
They live in Cranston. A word to the kid from me:
you dress like someone who lives on the Hill,
so lose that little leather jacket and the sneakers.
I don't think a nice girl from Cranston
would go around with someone like you.

Re: Mystery Girl at the Fountain   M4W — 28
Besides, you have a funny nose.

Re: Mystery Girl at the Fountain   M4W — 9
Thanks for defending me. But I like my jacket.
It's me. I don't think she, The Divine One,
cares one bit whether I'm wearing sneakers.
Can't anyone tell me her name, please?
Names mean everything! I want to write her a poem.

Re: Mystery Girl at the Fountain   M4W — 28
Poor kid, you got it bad. Her name is Beatrice.
Her mom calls her "Little Bea." Get over her.
You'll probably never see her again. In three years
all girls will look just as good to you.
Trust me on this.

Address for Mystery Girl, Please!   M4W — 9
This poster banned from Craigslist.
Code: Underage poster, inappropriate content

II — Five years later: Dan's Dairy

Feb 1 – No poetry yet this year. Life sucks.

March 1 — No poetry yet. Maybe I should just give up. Nothing good is ever going to happen to me.

March 14 — I can't believe my good fortune, or the coincidence. I saw Beatrice today, the Divine Beatrice. It's March 14. That's the same day we met five years ago.

 I was in Venda Ravioli and the church bell was ringing two. I always feel weird when I hear that church bell since it makes me remember *that moment*. I looked over, and there she was, one aisle away. I'd know her anywhere, though she is taller and now she has ~~boobs~~ breasts like all the girls in my class (only nicer). She was with two older women but I couldn't see them very well because of the way Beatrice *glowed*. There was a light around her. Not a halo, but a light all around her body. Funny that no one else seemed to notice.

 She was arguing with the women about which pasta to buy. They wanted to cook rigatoni and she wanted Angel Hair pasta. *Cappellini* it's called. "Look, mama," she said, "you can fit fifteen strands of cappellini inside a rigatoni."

 "What's that supposed to mean?" the woman I knew to be her mother asked. "And don't go opening the package to show me." She turned to the other woman and said, "This daughter of mine, she's allatime talking numbers. She counts and counts and counts." She held both packages and weighed them in her hands. "No difference," she argued. "They're both a pound. See the label?"

 And then Beatrice smiled and her eyes fixed on mine, and the tone of her voice changed so that I knew she was really speaking to me. Her exact words: "With the Angel Hair you get to eat 2.17 times more sauce."

 I was dumbstruck. I dropped a jar of the Mayor's pasta sauce. Everyone stared at me. What's worse, I didn't have enough to pay for a second jar and I got Hell from my mom. Hell is not something you want to go through often. And then Beatrice's mom made it worse. She pointed and laughed. "Isn't that the boy with the funny nose? Look how he's staring at you!"

 I don't remember what happened next.

I have to figure out what Beatrice meant.
So I made this drawing:

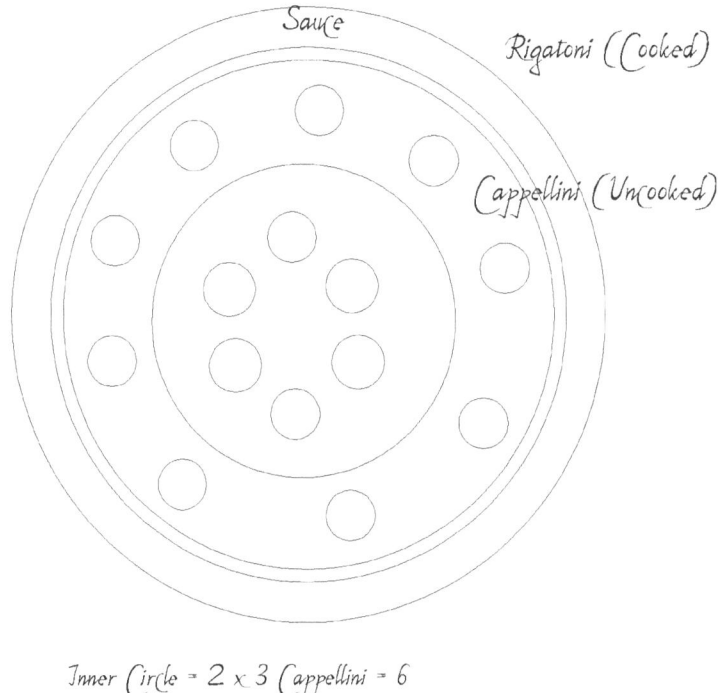

Inner Circle = 2 x 3 Cappellini = 6
Middle Circle = 3 x 3 Cappellini = 9
Outer Circle = 1 Rigatoni and Sauce
Circumfernece of Rigatoni = Pi x 0.680 = 2.14 inches
Circumference of Cappellini = Pi x 0.033 = .1036728 inches
Ratio of Circumferences: 21 Cappellini = 1 Rigatoni

The Cappellini are like planets. Two circles they form, one inner, one outer. Six in the Inner Circle, Nine in the Outer Circle. The Rigatoni surrounds them, just like the globe of stars surrounds the earth. I know this is important. She wanted me to figure it out. Three rings, three levels.

I asked my friend Guido C. (he's got a T-shirt shirt that says Shut Up About It – My Name Is Really Guido) to help with the math. How much sauce do you need to cover the outer pasta, and how much sauce do you need to cover 15 Cappellini? Guido says you have to use π (pi) to get the answer.

Guido's math, and what Beatrice said in the pasta store come out exactly the same! Beatrice knows π! She can do it in her head!

Last night I dreamt that someone was in my room. At first I thought it was Father Francis and reached for my baseball bat. But the figure just stood there. He told me: "Don't you see that π is everywhere? That all things, above and below, are connected by it?"

I woke up, and looked at my diary. I looked again. And then I saw it.

π is 3.14159, although the digits go on forever and never repeat. Six digits is all they make us learn in school. I met Beatrice both times on March 14, at 1:59 pm.

My love for Beatrice is like π.
π is irrational.
π is transcendental.
π never repeats.
π has no final point.
If there is a forever, it is bound by π.

Guido tells me: π to fifty places can calculate a circle the size of the known universe.

I don't know how much π defines the boundaries of Heaven or Hell.

At least not yet.

ARABESQUES ON EARLY MODERN MATHEMATICS

for Travis Williams

1
Somehow, before the zero,
the circle door into infinity
    via a nullity,
the world went about
its lucrative business.

Wealth was relative,
    untold riches,
    like Croesus or Midas,
    the sum total
     of all the tea in China.

Somehow, before the zero,
on toes and fingers, beads
    and the abacus,
with Byzantine rigors
of Roman numerals,
the profits were calculated,

the cost of carrying a fish on ice
from a stream in the Caucasus
to the Emperor's table
known every step of the way.

Somehow the counting houses
    counted, the censuses compiled,
        the taxes and tithes all gathered
in numbers inexact enough
    for each to slice a share
    along the way.

Until the subtle Arab zero,
    a lopsided egg, arrived.
Zero a placeholder,
    at first for nothing,
then, moving leftwards
    into hundreds, thousands,
stands for someone's
    possessing vast hordes
      of something.

Naught becomes aught,
    the aught implies the ought,
the obligation to pay
    the precise amount,
every counter counting
the same to the last drachma.
O miserable digit, as onerous
as Arab scimitars, shariah
of unforgiving digits!

2
Schoolboys now labored,
as though Greek and Latin
were not punishment enough,
on math, the museless art
beneath all trade and commerce.

This Arabized England
spewed forth unerring texts
applying number to space,
to time, to matter:

maps, ephemera of stars
and rising and falling moons,
aids to the perplexed farmer,
chemist and apothecary:
everything that was now had a number,

till Newton yoked number
to the Spheres Celestial,
poor Ptolemy disgraced and banished
so we might one day know
the price of a barrel of Saudi crude.

Even the land is subject to Number
as acres are measured and counted,
then coveted: the commons
enclosed, the poor
an inconvenient sum
to shift to another ledger:
the absorbent colonies.
Let them multiply themselves!

Primers were puzzle books,
    math without algebra,
absent symbolic thinking,
absent even the decimal,
    the fraction,
the answers whole numbers only:

easy to see the descent
   of a middling schoolboy
     from Greek to math
      to the madhouse,
shrieking a stillborn
   calculus in Bedlam,

while certain young women
whose minds did not wander
were set to task on tables
for each year's almanac:

high tides and low, sunrise and set
at each edition's latitude; tables
of weights and measures; days
to plant and harvest —
useful work, the knitting of numbers,
the loom of repetitive thinking.

3
There's no escape in Faith.
Who drew the first Saint's halo
presaged the Rome-world crowned
with the transcendent Zero,
an alien cuckold sign, a jest
against infinity and Trinity.

Trinity times Zero is Zero.
Trinity divided by Zero is Infinity.
The square root of Trinity
is an Irrational Number.
The straight and narrow,
the only line to heaven
is only the arc of an infinite circle,
the circle itself a Zero.

4
There is no escape.
Everything is nothing.
Your bank account is consumed
by zeroes, your numbered days
run down to zero like a bomb-tick.

You cannot knot the naught; it rolls
according to its own laws, its radius
locked to its outer measure
by the madness of pi. Ziggurats
of zeros, numbers' nebulae,
cosmos uncountable, columns
left, left, leftward until the number
expressed is more than the number
of anything that is or ever was or will be.
Still it does not end, this monster,
this all consuming *oh   oh   oh   oh!*

PEPPER AND SALT

    and I was only thinking
    about the shakers of salt and pepper
    that were standing side by side on a place mat.

    I wondered if they had become friends.
            — Billy Collins, "You, Reader"

Pepper and salt
are enemies:

chessmen on the place mat,
one black, one white,
forward-left, forward-right
political knights,
or plowing angular,
dissenting bishops
each to his heaven,
his rival to hell —

spill from one, a run
of bad luck;
spill from the other,
a sneezing fit
precipitate
of a heart attack.

Salt is poison
to pepper's ground:
no gardens grow
in Carthage, sown
with the sea's bitters;
no *papricum* in Sodom
where Lot's wife
stands petrified,
a mineral pillar.

If you are white,
all pepper is black,
a back-of-the-cupboard
kitchen mistress,
safely savored,
country of origin
unasked about,
milled, ground
to ash fineness.

If you are brown,
rainbows of spice
surround you:
cayenne, paprika,
jalapeño, chili,
hot on the tongue,
warm in the belly,
the edge of eros,
lips closing, teeth
bursting peppercorn,
sweat beads
across the forehead,
the supplicating smile,
the liquid eyes' surrender.

A Chinese chef,
wise in the way of things,
heats Szechuan peppercorns
till aromatic smoke
stings, fries salt
in the pepper's oil,
grinds all together
as "pepper-flavored salt."
His yin-yang craft subdues
two rival empires.

But here and now,
on this chrome-formica
dinner table, two
pale glass cylinders
stand separate,
monogrammed,
one "S" — one "P" —
imagine the horror
if P got into the S shaker! —
forever apart,
and no, not even
remotely friends.

SPOOL

A spool
    conceals a number,
    irrational
    and unrepeatable,
around which line
    becomes circle,
    spiral, around and up,
    then down again,
around which thread,
    or yarn, or twine,
    or wire or cable
acquire a memory
of curved space.
Flatten a wire —
    it springs back
    to coiled winding,
    snake-snarling itself
    into Medusa knots,
remembers its birth-winding,
its self-companioning
    a solipsist ellipse.

A spool on end
    is immobile,
its one eye heavenward:
a coffee house tabletop
    from cable reel,
stable as the Great Pyramid
for brim-full cups
    and dreamers' elbows.

A spool, overturned,
wheel-sided,
makes a run for freedom,
sees everywhere
    but where it's going
    and where it's been,
free-rolling wheels awaiting

one cat-paw out-thrust,
    the crazy captive twine
    chaos unraveling
    to feline delight.

Most spools unwind,
    yield up, forgetting,
discarding their cargo,
most spools are
    themselves discarded.
Some unwind, rewind:
    anchor cable,
    old tape recorder
        wire remembering
a Toscanini broadcast,
the spinster's patient rewind
    of unused yarn.

Some lives are spun out only,
unrecollected and barely lived;
some held in tight,
    the avarice of silk,
    the gold-leaf ribbon,
    the gauze bandage;

others ebb and flow:
    eyeline and lifeline
    cast to the elements,
withdrawn with fish-hooks,
    question-marks,
the empty space
    at spool's heart
recording, remembering,
never the same
two days in a row,
an endlessly varied integer
multiplied times *pi*.

ON A CHINESE FAN

On viewing a Chinese fan by Dong Gao at Christie's 2010[1]

Hand-painted, a universe of greens and grays
emerges from a background mist
on the sewn strips of a Chinese fan:
the scholar, a man of some wealth
and even greater erudition, has brought
(o wonder of labor and engineering)
a good half dozen scholar's stones,
each high as a house wall, soft stone
eroded to honeycomb by a millennium
of patient rain and hollowing,
forming three sides around his table;

at ease with his calligraphy, the brazier
bright and burning with water a-boil,
the servant refilling the *yi xing*[2] pot
as fast as he drinks down
the finest of water-nymph teas;
the reedy crooning of an *er-hu*[3]
fiddle at his right; off to the rear
a *pi-pa*[4] lute player awaiting
her turn to please him, the rocks
a perfect amphitheater;

birds hovering, pruned trunks
of trees on one side bending
the trunk in an artful curve
(how long it took to tease
one cherry in and among
the hollows of the *lingbi* stone!).[5]

---

[1] Dong Gao (1740-1818). The Chinese fan described here was sold at Christie's in 2010. The fan can be seen at:
http://www.christies.com/lotfinder/lot_details.aspx?intObjectID=5297928
[2] Yi xing, a red-purple clay used for making scholar's teapots and other ornamental ceramics.
[3] Er-hu, the two-stringed Chinese fiddle.
[4] Pi-pa, the Chinese lute
[5] Lingbi, name of the hollowed, perforated stone from Anhui province favored for scholar's stones.

No solitary scholar this,
alone in a gazebo perched
on some cliff above the cloud-line:
he has a secondary grove,
o'erhung with pine and willow
beneath whose shade
a table is spread with all his poetry,

where two friends tune the *zheng*,[6]
to whose melancholy fingerings
(glissando and tremolo)
they'll echo back his lines to him,
even while serving girls unwrap
the afternoon repast of tofu,
pickles piquant with rice vinegar
and red chilis, and red-bean cake.

Other friends ambulate
among the upthrust rocks
and clinging tree-roots,
catching the drift but not
the meaning of his poems
as wind and waterfall
hum through the sighing pines.

It is a place so beneficent
that in it poems are superfluous —

well, almost.

---

[6] Zheng, the Chinese zither.

THE LABYRINTH

There is only one way out
of this poem. You must walk
where I walk — the path
that a thousand have trod
before you. There is only
one way out of this poem.
All who have come this way
I have loved one way
or another. There is only
one way out of this poem.
Are you here because of beauty?
Or is it merely late night's
urgency? There is only
one way out of this poem.
There is a calm place,
after much losing of way,
the restful center where needs
and appearances cancel
each other in perfect stasis.
There is only one way out
of this poem. Others will follow.
I will mistake them for you
as I have mistaken you
for the form of the thing I want.
It takes as long to leave
as to enter; the center
provides no clue to escaping.
Two wings of one bird:
anticipation, memory.
There is only one way out
of this poem. Because I touch you,
you cannot retrace your steps.
You are not whom, or what
you were when you entered. There
is only one way out of this
poem. Here every lie is a monster,
every deceit a deceiver,

and truth is plucked from stones,
and the earth sings. There is
only one way out of this poem. Arms
down, extend your palms, feel it.
The power of earth-force Dionysian,
strong enough to lift you. There is
only one way out of this poem. Fly!

THE PERIODIC TABLE: HYDROGEN

You are the First One.
Once, your unity
was the Only Thing.
A hot blast of protons,
sperm stuff of the cosmos,
jostling your jillion
identical twins, up, down,
in a vibrant scream
of creative urges,
partnering in ions,
H dating H
(no law against it),

H_2 self-bonding,
converging in gas clouds,
gobbling stray neutrons,
dreaming of empire
yet eluding all,

stuff of the Ether,
the Bifrost stream
between galaxies,
ball lightning
and balloon flight,

ever at the edge
of an explosion
if oxygen is near,

holding your
secret of secrets dear:
the self-annihilating
self-fusion, the flame
at the heart of stars.

Without you, nothing;
with you, more questions
than ever answers,
light as a whisper,
    Hydrogen.

variations on eve

for Mary Cappello

eve is a palindrome,
its time-trough center
the intersect
of yesterday/ tomorrow

eve is always
fraught with magic:
budspring bonfires
on every hilltop,
virginal dreams
of future husbands,

witch brooms anointed
and flying,
Nutcracker abductions,
the false clarity
of first champagne;[1]

the eve of wanting
better perhaps
than the day of having;
the eve of counting
the dead who outnumber
our friends still living,
and all the more poignant
in its ripe wealth.

eve is a palindrome,
a boy-scratch icon
of two breasts
and a guess hazarded
of what's "down there."

---

[1] These two stanzas refer to May Eve, St. Agnes's Eve, All-Hallowed Eve (Hallowe'en), Christmas Eve and New Year's Eve.

eve is a palindrome:
in Milton's paradise,
self-seen in water,
then ripple, then
double-self, no —
it is Adam. Even
the metre is mirror'd
around eve's
solipsist *e*'s.

eve is a palindrome,
semiote of evil, Devil,
evolution's creation-crack,
Greek snake alarm
of *evohe! evohe!*
as if to say
"If woman comes,
can snake be far behind?"

"eve is a palindrome"
is in itself an anagram,
ten times varied:
Love me, in despair.
I, opal, seven-armied,
(ever a lapis *Domine*),
O Spire, leave a mind!
A love inspired me, a
piano, severed mail.
Are divine poems a reel,
a paved line? Is Rome
pined? Lo, *I* am a verse,
a palindrome. Is Eve?

ICE STORM

All of Rhode Island is covered in ice,
each tree and branch and branchlet
a candelabra; thousands of millions,
thousands of thousands of millions
of pearl-size gem-globes diamonding
the low December sun to nova brilliance —
countless as the stars in the visible sky —
    if tears, enough to count
    all the dead who ever died
    (Dante's innumerable rings
    of Hell and plateau'd Purgatory
    would not have space enough!) —
Niobe cried dry at last, relieved
of her weeping duty, calm
and at peace with her tormenter, Leto.

Ice spheres soften, elongate to cones,
tip to icicle spear-points and fall,
ring-singing their one-note, finite joy,
the unvoiced, voiced and visible,
their moment between two oblivions,
a self-made boat of water, westward
and down from iceberg to sea,
and so we sink, world ending with sun's
apocalypse, the blind and blinding
quotidian. We are never done with words;
picking up shards of thought, slip-
sliding way from our grasp as fast
as we can take them in hand,
the firm solitude of ice gone
in the melted pool of yesterdays.

LUCY: A VERSE MYSTERY

Vacant heart and hand and eye,
Easy live and quiet die.
                                   —Sir Walter Scott

I.
Providence, Rhode Island, 1848.
The bar in Poe's hotel, a proper bar
with deep mahogany paneling, row
upon row of wines to savor, great casks
of low-grade by-the-barrel rum, ales
unheard of except this close to the sea
that brought them — thumb-nosed and snug in the sight
of the disapproving First Baptist Church.
Let Roger Williams frown, the ladies
of the Temperance Society petition:
in vain since the long polished bar was lined
and elbow'd by half of the town's lawyers.
Rank upon rank of tables, niches and corners
sufficed for the lower sorts: workmen
in coveralls to the lean, carousing sailors
ear-ring'd in gold and of uncertain parentage.
Poe sat with Pabodie, a celebrated local,
a delicate man who had read at law
but had no taste for the practice, a poet

with a melancholy ode or two within him,
but above all a useful man, a man who knew
the nature of men and everyone's business,
a man to sound out about the Power family
whose elder daughter, a widow named Helen,
a poetess, he had come to woo.
An answer discreet affirmed her fortune
a small one, but reliable: property and mortgages,
well-managed by old Baptist lawyers.
Eyes rolled slightly around the bar
as Poe asked about the late Mr. Whitman:
a literary man, to be sure, a lawyer
who defended atheists and defamers
of preachers, a man of calamities
whose winter cold went pleural, and killed him.

And as for Sarah's father, "Ah, the less said,"
was all that Pabodie would offer. "And there's
a sister we don't speak much about." Poe felt
unable to pry more from Pabodie, at least
so long as he remained this sober. Gossip
is best pried with the lubricant of wine.
Poe talked instead of his earlier visit,
the summer of '45, of the moonlight
walk when he had seen Mrs. Whitman,
instantly his "Helen of Helens," behind
the red house in its snug garden, her hand
athwart the single rose she was cutting,
the sudden turn she made, her vanishing
into the cellar door whose soundless closing
stopped his breathing, as though to profane
this vision with any sound were unthinkable.
"I've sent her the poem with my recollection,"
he tells Pabodie, and shows him a copy.
Pabodie reads it and says: "Ah, lovely! A blank verse
paean to our finest poet. Her eyes — what lines! —
two sweetly scintillant Venuses! She will fall
into your power, rest assured, Mr. Poe."

"There was more to the poem," Poe confided,
"but I ought not frighten this Helen of Helens

with the thought of an apparition I saw,
or thought I saw —"

                          "An *apparition*?"
up went one of Pabodie's black eyebrows.
"You know their garden wall drops down
to the Episcopal churchyard, do you not?"

"I did not note it then."

                             "Tell what you saw,
and I will say if it has some common thread
with what *some* have said about that hillside
and what transpires at night there."

Poe turned over his manuscript, half-read
and half-invented as he spoke memory:
"But stay, pale Prophetess! Hold back the moon
And those hoarded clouds that would conceal it!
Return and calm my frenzied observing
Of a glowing form that rises — a form
I thought dead, that sleeps no more — it mounts
To speak its dread name into my hearing.
It spoke — not words in any human tongue! —
Thank God it did not speak *that name* or mine! —
A kind of half-whistled ululation.
Its eyes, two darkly luminous nebulae,
Caught mine, and sparked, and spurned me.
Then, folding in its shroud-like trail, it leaped
With superhuman will to the trellis,
Up, up, vertiginous, three storeys up
And either to roof or into attic
It vanished: all this in my one heartbeat
And in the darkness of one cloud's passing."

"What did you make of it?" asked Pabodie.
"You do not strike me, Poe, as a 'ghost' man."

"Ghosts, no! Place emanations, if you will,
or astral doubles our souls send out and just
as easily call back. Call them *wish forms*,
mesmeric force, all manner of ill-will:
there are many things in the universe,
and things we call to a semblance of life
by dreaming them or giving name." He paused.
"I fear the wine speaks now. Perhaps I say
too much and you think me but a madman.
I have made enemies with my science."

Pabodie smiled, and with a deft hand replaced
Poe's empty glass with its brim-full brother.
"What you have spoken of, we know quite well.
There are secrets we keep, and those we tell
because they amuse us and harm no one.
A spectre is haunting St. John's Churchyard.
Ask any of these gentlemen here — ask
and you shall hear the same tale from all."
Here Pabodie elbowed a young lawyer,
ushered him close to Poe for the telling:

"Sir, I could not but overhear. No lies
pass muster in this establishment, where friends
console and drink from sundown to midnight.
St. John's *is* haunted. I'll not be found there

on North Main on a moonless night; I'll not
look down there from Benefit Street above
if there's even a shadow in the place.
Just as you said, she comes in her own shroud,
hangs like a harpy in a spreading beech,
or spreads her tresses on a tabletop grave,
or darts from fence to yew to tombstone.
A harmless fairy, the sexton tells us
(but rum-full he sleeps, and never sees her).
They say her eyes can catch you, and once caught
you are lured to pass the night there, amid
the worms and moss and broken markers,
and if her eyes catch you, your life is hers
to do with as she pleases Night after night
she'll have you there for her pleasure, your pain.
Point out some wreck of a man in an alley
and all will say: 'Lucy has ruined him.'"

"Lucy?" Poe asked. "Why, of all names, Lucy?"

"That's what she calls herself. Sometimes she speaks
her name or a few lines of poetry."

Here Pabodie broke in, "And then she's gone,
as thin as smoke and pale as a firefly."

"So I have seen a spectre — the very same?"

"So, Mr. Poe, it would seem. I counsel you
to keep to yourself your summer vision.
The families on Benefit, you see,
have secrets, and keep them. Monsieur Dupin
would be hard-pressed to decipher them all."

Here Pabodie would say no more, but one
far voice from a distant table called out,
as an old sailor made bid to join them:

"Aye, that's Saucy Lucy y'er speakin o'.
She ain't no spirit, unless that 'spectre' word
is your gentleman's way of sayin' what

we all do see and know too well. Dark nights
she haunts the St. John's graveyard sure enough,
and if she catch your eye, an' it be late
and the sexton be well into slumber,
then many's the man that'ud go to her.
And as for doin' her biddin', that ain't
supernatural since she be wantin'
pretty much what the sailors be wantin'."

Pabodie paled and, finding a handkerchief,
shielded himself from the sailor's breath.
"I don't give credit to these bawdy tales,"
he said to Poe. "They hear — perhaps they see —
and to cover their fear they *embellish*."

Poe nodded. "For a gentleman, a ghost
suffices, a lonely ghost beyond all hope,
ephemeral, untouchable, some virgin
ripped from her life by contagion."
Poe stopped, choked, put out the glass
for another turn from the wine-cask.

II.
Past-midnight Providence was wide awake.
"The Raven" was requested, recited.
Then arm in arm he walked with Pabodie
to a Chinese laundry's doorway; from there,
having passed a yellow paper beneath it,
and waiting a seeming eternity,
the two poets entered a passageway
far into the hillside, into a damp room,
a ratty, fungoid, wet-walled warren
where a dozen reclining sleepers lay,
and beside them a dozen expiring pipes,
and Poe consented to stay.
When that was done, when dreams
beyond Coleridge, of galaxies borne
on a cosmic wind, of worlds created
from mere thoughts, and as readily destroyed
convinced him of his godhood, and madness —
and that was quite enough of that, he fled.

Alone as ever, and having walked
Mr. Pabodie to his High Street home,
Poe did what it was Poe's nature to do:
at every moment the most awful thing
he could think of. He stood, at last,
at the foot of St. John's churchyard.
And there were sounds, and with raven hair and
night-dark great-coat he passed for shadow
within shadow as he climbed the hill,
and he saw them, and what they were doing.
And the man fled. And the shrouded spectre
rose up from a cold lime table marker
and her white shroud billowed around her
and parted so she was full upon him
in her nakedness, a *lamia*, her eyes afire —
he felt her will like a maelstrom, insatiable,
unquenchable, to fall into her arms
like the nine-day fall into Hell, or the careen
into an empty grave. Her lips touched hot —
nails raked his neck — and Poe swooned dead away.

It was dawn when he awakened. In horror
he reached for his clothes about him
and found everything in place. His head
seemed under a great bell, his tongue
as stiff as an iron clapper, the taste
of rust, of iron, in his mouth; he wiped
and found blood there. He looked about
and spied no footprints on the damp earth
save those of his own zigzag ascent.
With Dupin's eye he surveyed all: the street
below, where one slow wagon was passing,
pulled by a somnolent mare; the high street
above the churchyard, seen only in gaps
between the garden walls and houses.
Only the shrubs and trees, and the darkness
of certain nights made this a private place.
His perverse imp had brought him here. And what
of the spectre? Did she hang even now
from some rooftop, or sleep beneath the lid
of a vaulted gravestone? No answers here,

but what was *this*? Poe strode to a gravestone
and found upon it a splendid binding,
a finely-printed edition of a book he knew,
"By the author of the *Waverly* novels" —
The Bride of Lammermoor. Lucy Ashton
is its doomed heroine: her first love lost,
she kills her bridegroom on her wedding night.
On the end leaf was an inscription, rubbed
out by an angry hand, and "S –A –P."

III.
"My mother, Mrs. Power." Poe bowed;
perhaps he bowed too deeply, perhaps
the bead-line of nervous moisture
across his brow betrayed him. He smelled,
not Muddy's faint rose, but camphor,
mildew and dampened woolens.
"We are honored to receive you, sir,"
the widow Power said stiffly.
"The honor is mine," Poe smiled, eyes lit
with the importuning son's mother-plea,
and she seemed to soften. He had not slipped.

Now Helen, her scarves aflutter, turned,
as another woman swept down the stairs
and into the dim-lit parlor. His hosts
seem startled. "My sister," spoke Helen,
"Miss Susan Anna Power." Poe bowed
as the slight figure, indifferently coiffed
and double-layered with a Chinese robe
thrown over a haze of many-layered skirts,
burst between Helen and her mother.
Poe bowed again. But silently, an awkward
suitor's pause on seeing a younger sister,
to outward view, an appropriate
deference to an unmarried woman,
but his inner voice spelled out:
Susan — **A**nna — **P**ower.

"The Raven has come to roost!" said Susan.
"The Raven comes to seize the dove —" The frowns
of Mrs. Power and Helen's consternation
were what they thought caused her to pause.
But no, she *spied the book* in Poe's left hand
against his charcoal-colored overcoat,
and flying across the parlor to him, as though
in salutation, half-bow, half-curtsey, she seized
the marble-edge volume, nails pressed
into the oak-brown leather with uncommon force.
She spoke in a sepulchral voice, so low
as to seem baritone, and from a distance:

"When the last Laird of Ravenswood
    to Ravenswood shall ride —"
To which Poe declined his head and answered:
"And woo a dead maiden to be his bride."
She parried "He shall stable his steed in the Kelpie's flow."
He ended, "And his name shall be lost for evermoe!"
And deftly, *The Bride of Lammermoor* passed
before the uncomprehending eyes
of the wooed one and the watchful mother.
And deftly, *The Bride of Lammermoor* passed
to *The Succubus of St. John's Churchyard*!

CHANCE CARDS IN THE WUTHERING HEIGHTS BOARD GAME

Pay $500 rent to Heathcliff.

Dogbite at Thrushcross Grange. Pay doctor $50.

Win $200 gambling with Hindley Earnshaw.

Heathcliff runs off with your sister. Lose inheritance.

Sleep with Linton Earnshaw or lose $100.

Name your child Linton Linton, Earnshaw Earnshaw, or Heathcliff Heathcliff.

Sleep in barn for two years. Forfeit $100 for porridge and breadcrusts.

Dig up Catherine Earnshaw. Collect $20 gravedigger's fee.

Lose Thrushcross Grange to Heathcliff.

Stay in Wuthering Heights forever.

SOMETHING THERE IS IN THE ATTIC

Every human body is a haunted house.
Something there is in the attic
that drives it and sets it course.
Are the shutters half-drawn?
Are they nailed against sunrise?
Do spiders spin in the tenantless rooms?
Who lives there? Ahab and his mono-
Moby madness? Emily with her dry-
leaf poems like money under a bed?
Or no one at all? Does no one hear
as each flaked shingle falls,
as varicose ivy beards up, as sun
and sag gray-wash the porch beams
and lintels? Something there is
in the attic that drives it and
sets its course. Whose will? An old
man's will? A boy's? A loud-mouthed
betrayer of dreams? A dreamer
paralyzed? Why does this house
not fall, but stand at elmward avenue,
accusing all, begging a moon,
a clean sweep, a neighbor's knock,
a letter? Something there is
in the attic that drives it and
sets its course. This house is
Ahab's ship, Usher's manse, Lovecraft's
infirmary, a witch house, feast
hall, love nest and chapel, sanctum
of Solitude, the Capulets' tomb.
If every human body is a haunted
house, shall we not choose
these ghosts? Can I not summon
a typing poltergeist, a coloratura
howler, a phantom raconteur
to teach me all dead languages,
a gourmet chef insomniac,
someone for whom the *1812 Overture*
has not (as for me) ever lost its charm,
a friend who hovers over Batman comics

and knows every line poor Bela Lugosi
was ever made to utter. Room enough,
and beds, and food and tea, for them all!

In October this house is avalanched,
as leaves, and ghosts of leaves
from every tree that ever crisped
in the tug between slant-sun and frost,
pile high in ziggurats of oak,
maple and sumac, hawthorn and willow,
each with a tale of hope and sorrow
waiting its turn for harvest.
They almost obscure the house, so high
that one lone cupola, the poet's watch,
stands apex at its pyramid,
as one mad vane whirls at the whim
of indecisive winds, as lightning rod
trembles for discharge of the weighted sky
into the attic haunter's cranium.

I am that attic Something: I drive
this house unchanging, wall-to-wall
with mad cargo. My gambrel roof
is an upside-down Mayflower
as I sail against the leaf-tide. Monsters
would block my passage: great whales
of Doubt breach above a maple current;
the baleful skyward eye and tentacles
of the giant squid of Loneliness float by
in a sea-tide of weeping willow.

Yet something there is in the attic
that billows the sails, and drives me on.
The madness that fills these pages
is self-sustaining: some days
these scratchings seem meaningless,
unmusical; some days I read and gasp
and shudder to think that somehow I wrote
or was written through, to reach this apogee.

Alone? Well, lacking the guests
I crave, I must split and become them.
Books, cat and bed, a galaxy of music,
teapot that fills as fast as I empty it:
it is not a bad life,
to be the haunter of one's cobwebbed self.

THE VANISHED CHAPEL

Back for a holiday some years ago, I visited
my college home, that old Episcopal chapel,
whose attic garret I lived in
(scandal unheard-of in those days,
an atheist-poet-pervert
doing who knows what under the eaves)

It was just a year after I fled to New York.
I walked the new tenant over the grounds,
hidden behind white clapboards,
I had gardened two summers.
"Here," I say "are the onions, back
from last year — I planted these.
A little ground fire in spring
will weed through those blackberries,
in summer they'll go to eight feet.
The sod here is cleared, for last summer
I took shovel and planted peas, lettuce,
carrot, red radish. Rabbits, oh yes,
they ate the peas right down to the ground.
A sour kind of clover, *oxalis* I think it's called,
grows here on the lawn,
boon to salads. Wild flowers,
good for a week in the house."

(By the wall, a garrulous stalk,
alien seed pods clumped in the sun,
six feet of rhubarb — don't know
who planted the stuff. Even the kids
    keep away, too much
resemblance to Body Snatcher pods.)

A year passed. I visited again.
The tenant was gone, they told me.
The grocer's kind,
    he ate no onions, left
    the berries for birds;

They covered the yard with gravel,
   nothing there but dandelions
      and cars.

Decades passed. I came again
and hardly recognized the spot.
The chapel had gone to ruin, then burned.
The garden is a weed-lot. Trees,
already thick and sturdy, assert
the primacy of forest. One more place
I have lived in, obliterated. How long
did the chapel stand empty, shunned,
the object of lingering rumors
of things that went on in that attic?

How many come back, to look and remember,
not the Episcopal mumbling
that went on downstairs, but the mad
poetic ramblings and strange seductions
that made the attic infamous,
mad nights that nearly rove the roof off
as Wagner and Shostakovich, Mahler and Bach
roared and rattled the windows
and sent the single bat (too poor for a belfry)
aflutter, then out the open casements?
Whatever became of the church-bulletin mimeo
that doubled as printing press
for our underground newspaper?
Oh, the thought of my old mattress in flames,
site of so many dreams and conquests!

Churches come. Churches go.
The poet in the attic remains.

HUMORESQUES

A NIGHT IN EDDIE'S APARTMENT

for Eddie Rivera

The front door tells you everything:
it is not square, but cut
to the angle of the attic roof.
The outside doorknob, once pulled,
stays in your hand —
its partner, somewhere inside,
rolls down the long hallway.

Eddie gives me the quick tour
with its Paterson caveats:
drink only filtered water;
check the expired dates
on anything in the refrigerator.
Enjoy the TV and stereo —
here's a complete set
of *Girls Gone Wild*.

And in the loo,
if you do Number Two,
chase every flush
with a bucket of water.
Things just don't stay down.
There is no telephone,
but next to the bed
he leaves me a potato peeler
in case of intruders.
"Just gouge an eye out,"
he advises me.

I am alone all night,
 but this place is haunted
 by Eddie's absence.
He does not sleep here much
 since *she* came along.

I snoop the bookshelves and CD racks.
From his cassette era I spy
   a dusty gospel section
   Praise Band and Jesus Power.
This stuff gathers dust now,
while the DVDs called
Latina Lovers and
Big Natural Tits 9
show signs of frequent viewing.
Finr and good,
but where are those
Ricky Martin videos?

I take a long bath,
grow drowsy, think I hear
voices in the bedroom.
No one is there:
only a comforting pile
of stuffed animals —
raccoons and pandas,
a pink elephant,
their mouths stitched shut.
The radio is silent.

Then an unholy clatter
begins in a dresser drawer.
Buzzing and bumping
and a kind of slobby fumbling.
I open the drawer —

the *Pleasure Her Now*
battery vibrator
has somehow joined up
with the Dr. Johnson
oral stimulator,
its latex and tubing
now totally merged
in yin-yang completion.
The latex lips
of the oral stimulator smile
and it says,

"We don't need him anymore.
Tell Eddie he can go to hell!
Now leave us alone!"
I snap the drawer shut.

I sleep fitfully. I still
hear voices muttering, moaning.
I awake in moonlight
slice-diced through venetian blinds.
I am not alone now:
a perfect circle of animals
has formed on the bed around me.

"It's him," the panda says.
"How can you tell?"
    the pink elephant snarls.
"You only have buttons for eyes."
"It's not him,"
the raccoon sniffles.
"He always puts us
under the covers at night."

"I don't care!"
the white rabbit
remonstrates.
It leaps on my chest,
and its carrot-breath
contralto pleads,
"*Amor de mi vida!*
Take me, Papi!"

I hurl the rabbit away,
run for the bathroom,
turn on the light.
Down in the toilet bowl,
something is moving.
A brown head peeps out
from the undercurve of pipe.

I think I see
a single baleful eye.
A shrill voice addresses me:
"Just tell Eddie
there's no use running away.
Tell him he can't
get rid of us that easily.
Tell him we're all
down here waiting."

I do *two* buckets of water,
two flushes
before I go back
to face the animals.

That's when the pink elephant,
the white rabbit's lover,
came at me
with the potato peeler.

I sat till dawn
in Dunkin' Donuts.

THE ADVENTURES
OF SOCK-PUPPET PETER

for A.F.

1
In a Tokyo laundromat,
atop an unclaimed bag,
Sock-Puppet Peter
watches his mute, deaf, blind
brethren toss and tumble
in the hell-heat of a spin dryer.

Some, he knows, will not survive
the ordeal: some snagged
on hook or zipper, some bleached,
out at the toe or heel.
Some, having lost their partners,
will allow themselves the indignity
of becoming dust rags.

The boy, a very devil,
a young Frankenstein, made him,
sewed on two button eyes,
scruffed and electrified him
into a semblance of life,

more fun to be with,
the boy insisted,
than the family dog,
Peter, at least, can talk me to sleep.
He's there on the pillow
when I awaken. I can take
him everywhere.

Worn as a sock,
peeping at edge of high-top
sneakers, smuggled in underwear,
a sinister bulge
withdrawn in giggle fits,

snug under mitten,
sock-puppet Peter
is a master of disguise.

Till suddenly, the house
is a whirl of packing, clothes
thrown into steamer trunks,
the dog into a hermetic shell
bound for the cargo hold,
sock-puppet Peter tossed in
to the last day's laundry —

a day, a week, a month
as cherry blossoms come
and fall, till friends
of the laundry owner pick over
the linens, the underwear,
until he, the last of the last, watches,
a limp-lorn Butterfly,
as others' captive hosiery
tumble and toss in the dryer.

One day the laundryman finds
the errant laundry ticket, exclaims:
"Gone, all gone now.
Family gone to Vienna!"

2
Sock-Puppet Peter
smuggles himself
by diplomatic pouch
from Tokyo to old Vienna.
He reads everything
in the case around him:
The Michelin Guide to Vienna,
The CIA Area Guide to Austria,
Teach Yourself German
(not sure how a sock
can deal with umlauts),
and a useful anthology
of East Europe's most troubled

fiction writers.
Sock-Puppet Peter
is riveted by Gogol's "The Nose,"
Kafka's *The Metamorphosis*.
He dreams of finding
lost attributes:
a clerk's nose,
a more convincing eyeball,
a few spare legs
from a centipede, maybe.

He crawls to the clinic
of Dr. Sigmund Freud (alive
after all these years and wars!)
stretches himself out
on the famous sofa,
relates his recurring dream
of loss: that white,
five-fingered hand
he had once enveloped,
the sense of being moved
and spoken through.

"I'm not sure I can help you,"
Freud speculates,
"You never had a mother.
You never saw
    your little sister naked, you say.
You don't miss
    having a penis, you tell me.
Und zo, let us talk
    about the time you spent
    down the boy's trousers…"

3
Sock-Puppet Peter
is banished from the Prater
for eating a carrot
"suggestively," they said
in the police report.
Released in the care
of his psychiatrist,
he lunches with Freud,
who wants to know everything.
"What did your jailers do to you?
Did you dream in your cell,
and, if so, about what?
Did anyone, when lights were out —"
Freud licked his dry lips expectantly,
"Did anyone, you know...?"
Freud orders schnapps
and Wiener Schnitzel,
Peter a knockwurst special.
"Eat, my young friend, eat,"
Freud waves him on.
"They must have starved you
    in that jail cell!"
Peter begins eating.
Freud watches horrified
as the sausage end vanishes
into sock-puppet gullet.
This will clearly take a while,
like the anaconda's slow intake
of the struggling victim.
The sausage slip-slides
from sock mouth, to plate,
back into sock mouth.
Between the masticating noises,
Peter hums a Strauss Waltz.
"Don't ever do that
in my presence!" Freud cries.
pulling the plate away.
"That's disgusting!
No wonder they arrested you!"

The waiter comes over, alarmed.
"Herr Docktor Freud,
the diners are complaining.
We'll have to ask you to leave now."
"My patient's bad manners,"
Freud stammers. "I'm not responsible!"
The waiter replies icily:
"What patient, Herr Docktor Freud?
that's *your* arm, in that old sock,
making obscene gestures with a sausage."

The knockwurst falls. Freud rips off Peter
from his extended arm, hurls him
onto the back of a shawled lady,
who huffs away oblivious.
Out, out the double doors, wind lifts
Sock-Puppet Peter onto the back of a taxi,
where he clings, gasping,
making his getaway.

4
Sock-Puppet Peter
sits on a park bench,
next to a playground,
stretches himself out
to take the sunlight.
What does Freud know,
anyway, the old fool,
fishing about for mother memories?
Now, maybe someone,
some passing child,
would pick him up,
enter him eagerly,
give him a new name
with no police record.
A red-haired boy,
nanny trailing, sees him.
"A puppet, Mathilde!
May I have it?" *Yes, yes.*
The chlorine-smelling hand

of the nanny lifts him. *Not you.*
The boy, the boy!
"A filthy thing, Hans!
Who knows where's it's been?
It smells like spoiled meat."
She flings him away
with the tip of her umbrella
into a tangle of shrubbery.

Sock-puppet Peter
dangles from twig and leaf,
rain-sog and night-fog.
He's aromatic
of mildew. If
buttons could weep, if
the faint crease
that had once been a mouth
could call for help —

calling, cawing,
two ravens find him,
pick at the button thread —
one eye is gone! —
pull at the frayed spot
where once a big toe —

oh! not like this,
unraveled, unwoven,
ending his life
as a bird-nest lining!

Sock-puppet Peter
pulled this way, that way
by raven talons,
torn free, high-flying
above the treetops,
across the Wienerwald,
over the slate-top roofs,
the Musikverein,
the Imperial palaces —
ah! the Danube!

He is pulled to the limit
of cotton-orlon,
this way, that way —
then shadow,
    blackness,
    beak-scream
    and blood-splash —

Thank the hawk
that rammed midflight
the stunned ravens,
the breeze
that caught Peter
and curled him down,
leaf-light
onto the parapet
of the Donau Bridge.

5
Hundreds walk by,
thousands, even.
His one eye
implores them
for a home,
a gentle sudsing,
a seamstress.

He's too much like
the sooty pavement,
the wrought-iron railing.
In vain his eye
tries winking, weeping.
His rent toe twitches
into the semblance
of puppet mouth,
but neither *Meinherr*
nor *Fraulein*
escapes him.

A bearded man,
who might be Dr. Freud
averts his eyes
and passes,
his low voice muttering
>   *I must not, must not*
>   *think of ferns. Of ferns*
>   *I must not think . . .*[1]

What odds,
   as autumn rolls on,
of meeting a man
   with one sock missing,
a child desirous
   of a Cyclops puppet,
a kindly spinster
   who could darn and sew,
  mine her button box
   for a matching eye?

Three idling boys
with skateboards,
linger at bridge-end,
searching new surfaces
for flight and fall,
gravity's iconoclasts.

Sock-puppet Peter
resolves to end it.
The Danube is rising
as full moon emerges
from cloud-clot.
He edges himself,
inch-worming the rail
till he is poised,
only his eye and toe-tip
upward, his damp weight
dragging downwards.

---

[1] Freud suffered from an uncontrollable fear of ferns.

Only a few seconds now,
as one of the boys —
    moon catches face —
        it's *him*, it's *him!*

He reaches out —
    a hand! that hand! —
        "My sock! My puppet!
            I left it in Tokyo!" —

and Peter falls,
    black cloth twirling
        to inky blackness
and Peter cries   and the boy cries

    N   N
    O   O
    o   o
    o   o
    o   o
    o   o
    o   o
    o   o
    .   .
    .   .

H. P. LOVECRAFT AT THE NEWSSTAND

on seeing a Justin Bieber special issue of US Magazine

COLLECTORS' EDITION

SIX HOT
POSTERS INSIDE!

H. P. LOVECRAFT:
MY
PRIVATE
WORLD

Exclusive photos
inside my bedroom

My New
Letter-Writing
Life

How I Cope
With Being Unknown

WIN!
A TRIP
TO MEET
HOWARD.

South Pacific Nightmare:
Edward and Bella
Breakup —
Eddie Storms Out
Over Howard-Bella
R'lyeh Love-Nest.

Online:
Howard Lovecraft Totally Naked OMG!

New Howard Lovecraft
Six-Pack Abs.

More Howard Shirtless Pictures
Click Here.

Howard and Sonia —
Our Embarrassing
First Date:
Young Author Panics
At First Sight of Spaghetti.

"He was An Ugly Baby":
Howard's Mom Tells Diary
In Weird Rant
From Butler Hospital.

First Photos:
HOWARD IN RIO!
Grandpa's Coat by Day;
Wig & Mom's Dress
For Carnival.

HPL Signs On
For Reality Show:
"The Whateleys,"
Won't Talk
About Howard's
Attic Room-Mate.

Teen Alert As Nuns
Seize Lovecraft Volumes:
Why Believing In Cthulhu
Means You're
Not Catholic.

Death Watch After
Lovecraft Shocker:
My Thirty-Year Addiction
To $C_{12}H_{22}O_{11}$.
"This Quadrant of Pie
Is My Last."

BALLET OF THE HORS d'OEUVRE

The gentlemen down front
at the Opera House,
the pretended balletomanes
who crowd the best seats
for calf- and leg-views,
brood over the program.

Tonight's dance interval
amid the modernist opera's
banging and clanging is — what? —
Ballet of the Hors d'Oeuvre.

"Horse Doovers?" asks one.
"Whore's Works!" another,
adept at translation (he is, after all,
an international banker) says
assuredly. A third,
the monocled one, harrumphs
and simply pronounces
"*Or derv*, gentlemen,
as in — appetizers."

A welcome roll from the timpani
muffles the disgrace
of the top-hat tycoons
as the ballet commences.
The music is, thank God, melodic.

First come the celery sticks,
vaguely aphrodisiac,
stalking on stage in stiff
march time, leaf-fringed
and vertical, tilting in time
to the Danse Crudité
and deftly choreographed
considering the absence
of any visible eyes.

As if to mock men's
expectations of limbs exposed,
two dozen chicken wings
crab-walk in unison
from left to right, then
right to left, then leap
into a wagon, a heap
of unappealing angles,
pulled off the stage
by a Harlequin cat.

Seedless grapes tumble
to a fast gigue
around a gaggle
of dowager strawberries,
the vast Chernobyl kind,
red-rouged, bewigged
with vernal leafage,
plump and no doubt
devoid of any trace of flavor.

To a Chinese flute, squat
four-lobed dumplings arrive
tip-toe on red shoes
scarcely visible
beneath the deep-fried
ballooning gowns.

Slow sarabanding,
the Crabs Rangoon
accelerate to dervish
then spin off stage.

A Danse Génerale
of crackers, round and square,
pair off against various
cheeses in national attire
raising the whole affair
to a Tchaikovskian frenzy.

Skirts fly, thighs bulge, as,
cubed, sliced, and quartered,
yellow and white, blue and orange,
they whirl and pair, unpair and tease
the desperate and crumbling crackers.

Then, finally, a show of stage magic
as each cheese maid slides through
the narrow blade of a slicer
and emerges as two likenesses,
whirling accelerando
until every Tilsit, Gouda,
Cheddar and Blue
meets her destined cracker
and goes obscenely
horizontal.

The front row gentlemen
are beside themselves
as the curtain falls.
What to do until the third act?
Backstage in the Green Room
where the undressing, redressing
ballerinas pretend not to be watched
by the drooling financiers,
what was one to do?

"I suppose," the monocled one hazards,
"although we're not even sure
which were the ladies,
we could go back for a nibble."

THE NEW TENANT

It's silent below
in the Army/Navy warehouse
when the second-floor tenant
tunes up his tweeters,
fires up the thunder
of a mammoth subwoofer.
(Dim-lit, mouse quiet, the attic's
an atelier of art school women,
bed squeaks, drain gurgles,
keys in the lock
their only aural assertion.)

On Floor Two, it's Beethoven:
Egmont and Equestrian Marches,
answered from below
by jackboots *ein-zwei* goose-stepping,
old army uniforms'
starched arms saluting.

When it's the *Marseillaise* above,
a hundred French sailor suits,
enfants de la Patrie,
fly from their hangers below,
and flap an apache dance
against the window panes.
(A teapot whistle,
summarily stifled,
a stainless steel spoon
clabbering porcelain
the only sounds
from the attic.)

On Shostakovich night
the orchestra thunders:
below, old Stalin medals
and Lenin pins skitter,
while *CCCP* tee-shirts
puff up angrily.

A Russian army greatcoat
stuffs its pockets
with an ever-growing list
of local citizens
with anti-People tendencies.
(The attic is dark
as a desanctified belfry.)

When he crescendos up
to the *1812 Overture*,
trunk-tops flip open below:
landmines and hand grenades
roll about aimlessly,
their impotent collisions
no match for cannons,
the clangor of church bells.
(While "Bowling for Hitler"
plays on the floor below,
the artists above
tip-toe in fur-lined slippers,
each in her own I-pod,
ear-bud solipsism.

On a more somber night
he has tea and listens
to Britten's *War Requiem*.
A solemn tramping erupts
onto the stairwell.
There is a knock. He looks
into an eyeless socket,
a leering skull,
an armless doughboy jacket,
not one, but the first
of a long line
of crutched and crippled
soldier semblances.

"Pucelles?" the coat-ghost asks.
"Frauleins? Girls?"
Cocking an ear
to the faintest sound
of a hair dryer,
the tenant points upward.
The tramp-tread of dead boots
mounts to the third floor.

The art school girls
have visitors.

TWO PHILOSOPHY STUDENTS

Randall's umbrella is tatter-torn,
bare spokes inviting leaf-catch or lightning.
Rain pelts his hair, his eyes
    swell shut with sea-brine.
He thinks a thought-wedge
against the wrenching wind:

    this thing above me possesses the *form*
        of an umbrella,
    therefore it must *be*
        an umbrella.
    Therefore, I am dry.

Sleet pounds his brow to migraine.
His soiled jeans get a needed washing.
He asks himself: What constitutes
"the Wet" as opposed to "the Dry?"

In lightning flash,
Armando passes Randall,
the wind to his back,
stooped as always,
his shapeless gym bag
weighted with something
the size and shape
of a bowling ball.

His back-pack, drenched now,
contains the yellowed pages
of his doctoral thesis,
begun a dozen years ago.

He sleeps in a carrel
on Level 3 of the Library,
a spot behind a stairwell
that no one ever enters.

There he will dry himself,
thumbing through Heidegger,
warming his dissertation
from log to turning sheets again,
his gym bag unzipped
to display the head
of his advisor,
gone on sabbatical
some years now
but never missed.

Armando does not like
these rainy afternoons.
The head seems heavier,
smells ever so slightly
as he shuffles upstairs
to the cobwebbed stacks
somewhere between
Metaphysics and Ontology.

AUTUMN ON MARS

for Ray Bradbury

On Mars, the black-trunked trees are dense
with summer's crimson foliage.
When dry-ice autumn comes,
the oaks there singe sickly green.
The land is a riot of airborne olive,
    chartreuse and verdigris,
green fire against a pink and cloudless sky.
The sour red apples go yellow sweet;
the wind-blanched wheat
    forsakes its purple plumage;
cornstalks are tied in indigo bundles;
eyes flicker ghoulishly
    as candles are set
        in carved-out green gourds.

Grandfathers warn their terrified children
of the looming, ominous blue planet,
roiled with thunderclouds and nuclear flashes,
that warlike, funeral-colored Earth
from which invaders would one day come,
decked in the somber hues of death,
withered and green like dead-pile leaves,
armed to the hilt with terrible weapons.

"I've seen them!" an elder asserts.
"They have two eyes, flat on their heads!"
Eye stalks wiggle in disbelief.
"They walk on two legs, like broken sticks!"
Multijointed leglets thump in derision.
"They speak in the animal octave,
    and they bark like krill-dogs."
The children shriek in red and purple.
"No way, Old One! Don't make us think it!
How can they talk without twinkling?"

"Their rockets go higher with every turn
    of our world around the life-star.
Earthers will come, thick on the ground
    like our thousand-year mugworms.
They will kill us, take our females captive,
burn our egg domes, eat our aphidaries!"
A fireball slashes the pink horizon.
Two hundred eye-stalks follow the arc.
"That might be one of their robots now!
Their probes are watching everywhere!"
Now fifty Martian youngster scream,
shrieking in ultraviolet tones,
crab legs scattering in every direction.

The Old Ones smile in five dimensions,
sit down for a cup of hot grumulade
and some well-earned peace and quiet.
"It's not nice to frighten the young ones,"
the eldest muses, "but it wouldn't be autumn
without a little Halloween."

TWO VERSE PLAYS

CARLOTA, EMPRESS OF MEXICO

Carlota's Ghost. Etching by Riva Leviten.

DRAMATIS PERSONAE

Carlota, ex-Empress of Mexico (1864-67), daughter of Leopold, King of Belgium, widow of Archduke Maximilian of the House of Habsburg. A short, thin woman appearing to be in her late seventies, but actually in her late eighties.
Marie, her maid (non-speaking part).
The visitor, an attractive young woman in her twenties, a 1920s look in her attire, but with conservative make-up and hair-do. (Non-speaking part. The visitor may be portrayed, or may be invisible. If the visitor is not portrayed, Carlota speaks to the audience as though it were the Visitor.)

THE SETTING
A darkened sitting room in the Chateau de Meysse in Belgium, late spring or early summer, 1927.

SCENE, FURNITURE, AND PROPS

This play may be formed with a bare stage and simple lighting, leaving it to the viewer's imagination what is real and what is a figment of Carlota's imagination. If it is fully staged, the following provides a description of the set and the necessary props:

One window stage right, is heavily curtained, with a blind that can be raised to admit some sunlight. Next to the window, a small table with a periscope-type viewing device, or a hand telescope, which can be used to look out the window unobserved.

Off center on the stage is a raised dais with a heavy antique chair positioned to simulate a throne. Carlota, Empress of Mexico, is seated on the throne, in a threadbare black dress. She adjusts a diamond tiara. There is a small table to one side of her throne, containing a large, clear glass bowl full of water and fake diamonds, rubies and emeralds. The table has a drawer (inside are parts of a black-hair extension – the side curls she uses to recreate her "Mailand" hair-do from the 1860s.) The Empress frequently wets her hands in the bowl, stirring around the "gems" at the bottom. Two smaller chairs: one next to Carlota's throne seat, the other, a high-backed chair, where the unseen visitor is directed to sit.

At stage center, behind Carlota's throne, is a large folding screen. The top of a white crinoline gown hangs over the screen, as does part of a fancy black shawl. An old traveling valise is also partially visible. Near the screen is a small dresser, containing a hand-mirror.

A grand or baby grand piano at stage left.

At stage left, one or more doors, through which the visitor, and the maid, Marie, will enter.

CARLOTA
(Sifting through her jewels in the water bowls, stopping to inspect some. Outside, the sound of a car approaching on a gravel roadbed. It stops, car doors open and close. Footsteps on gravel, faint. Carlota looks to the window, then hurries over with a swift, birdlike movement. From a small table, she unfolds the "periscope" and inserts it between the window blind and the glass. She withdraws it with a snap and folds it up, returning it to the table.)

(Loudly) Marie! Marie! A motorcar! Men in black! Intruders!

(Listens for an answer. In the distance, a doorbell rings. Carlota freezes for a moment, then, in the manner of one repeating a well-practiced checklist, hurries to the traveling valise. She kneels quickly, opens the valise and peeks inside to be sure of its contents, then snaps it shut. With a great deal of effort, she stands and then returns to her throne. She pats her white hair, which is tied back tightly, then takes a gray-colored bonnet from the side table and fastens it over her head. She waits silently for a moment, then calls again:)

Marie! Marie! Who is it? At the gate?
Why was no one there, watching at the gate?

(Several beats of silence. Carlota turns to the audience, shakes her head.)

Servants! What use are they? *(Listens.)* Ah! On the stairs.
That's Marie. Another — and a light step —
not boots, thank God! not those soldiers again!

(Straining to see).

Ah, Marie! And our visitor. Welcome! *(Remembering the appointment, she hastily removes the bonnet, revealing her tiara).*
(In French) Bienvenu a notre prison! *(In German)* Wilkommen auf Irrenhaus! *(Laughs)*
Prison and madhouse for sixty long years!

(Marie enters and curtsies, then moves aside to prepare tea.)

Come forward, my dear. The Countess has said
your French is exquisite, your reading voice
a pleasure to the ear. I need to hear
some German, too, if you could read to me
the journals from Berlin and Vienna.
Do you speak Spanish? Not a word, you say?
A shame, but I have my Marie for that;
she's been with me since Mexico, in fact.
Sometimes at night we read our Cervantes.
and I have all the histories here: monks
    and conquistadors, plunderers and priests —
Oh, I have not forgotten Mexico,
Cortez to our days at Chapultepec.
Empires gone, and this endless waiting game.

    I should compose a *memoir?* A kind thought.
    I have been asked. Writers and editors
    besieged me — I never once answered them.
Now I am too old for correspondence —
my secretaries are pensioned away.
I need youth, intelligence, about me.
I am far from finished. — And you, my dear,

Your time with me here may pass with pleasure —
Though I am mad, *(laughs)* I am not angry much,
except at kings and Popes and thievery.
We shall have tea, and spend *l'après-midi*
becoming acquainted. I love Chopin —
I hear you play the melancholy Pole?
No modesty, please! I hear you play well,
with passion if not precision — who cares
if the notes are right if the soul burns bright?

But I'll not demand a daily concert.
Some days you'll come to me and simply read,
but when it rains I yearn for some music.
I'm mad for Berlioz, whom no one favors now.
His *Trojans at Carthage!* a masterpiece!
(How well I know Queen Dido's tragedy!)
Berlioz would love our Mexican opera,
a house as fine as any in Europe.

I wanted to commission him (fiery,
a red-haired man) an epic opera —
our history from Aztec to Empire —
Montezuma's betrayal, the dreadful
ravaging Spaniards, the Pope
and his twisted Inquisitors —
what a *Marche Macabre* that would make
      (stops, holds out her hand)
do I offend you, my dear? —

(To Marie, who has brought a tea tray, indicating a position in front of her).
                             Here, Marie,
put the tea before me so I may serve it. —

You're blushing, my dear. I'm no Bolshevik.
I was a *Catholic* majesty once.
The Pope blessed us all, Max and Carlota,
the French army, the sailors — the guns, too!
I thought those millions of poor Indians
were souls to save — I did not know the Cross
was on their necks, crushing them. And the priests!
fat, bloated things like overfed spiders!
Look! Marie bristles at my blasphemy,
but here I sit, unblasted. Pius, dead!
So many dead. Half of Europe is dead.

(A beat, reconnecting her train of thought.)
Enough! We were talking about Berlioz.
But he is gone now, too. Poor Berlioz,
hounded by fools out of his own Paris.

(Pouring the tea into two cups)

Here's tea! *Chinois* or *à l'anglais?*
My preference, too! *¿Y con azucar?*
How many lumps, I mean. Tea is too good
for the English, a bilious brew chalked up
with a cow's milk to mask its bitterness.
This tea comes annually from China

with a note from their mission in Brussels.
After all these years, they remember me!

Come sit here, closer — no! take *this* chair —
the one on my right is Max's always.

Marie! More light for our visitor.

(Marie adjusts the window to admit more light.)

We'll draw the shade up just a little bit
so I can see her better. A fine face!
You should make a good match at someone's court —
Ah! if there were any left in Europe!
Mon Dieu! Who's left? Nineteen-Twenty-Seven!
My invitation list is a shambles,
a catalog of graves and asylums.
No chandeliers and ballroom mirrors *here*:
we must have blinds and double curtains drawn
always against those would-be assassins,
against the sight of those terrible birds.
Did you see them? You shall, my dear. You shall.

(Reaches for the newspaper on the tea table.)
Here is *Le Monde*, and somewhere, not here,
a German novel I would have you read from.
Yes, we will need more light for when you read.

(Carlota sips tea, then puts her cup down and distractedly runs her hand through one of the bowls of water. The colored gemstones drop from her hand into the water)

Rubies and emeralds, yes hidden here
in plain sight. I am too old to wear them.
The diamonds are almost impossible to see.
As gypsies do, I keep my gems about.
I might just need them, at any moment,
to buy my freedom, or rescue my Max.

We are not so remote as one may think.
Those armies are just a train ride away.
Back in the Great War the Kaiser's soldiers
marched right behind our garden walls!
They tried to requisition the chateau's
produce — all the gardens, the hens, the cows.
Remember those gray and tasteless bread loaves
they tried to offer us, Marie? Thank God
for Mr. Whitlock's American touch
that got us back our house immunity.
The Germans dared not enter a Habsburg house!

I slept in a traveling garb for months —
my portmanteau was always ready for flight.
The bombs, the lights, the men, the gas — *mon Dieu*!
That's when I remembered the good advice
my grand-mama once gave me at seven:
"Always have on you some trinket or gem
valued enough to pay for your honor,
or poison sufficient to avenge it."
I knew such things, and all the lineage
of the thrones of Europe, before I knew
that women bleed. The tea is cold, Marie.
Send to the kitchen for more hot water.

(Marie puts her hands on her hips in exasperation. It is obvious from the gesture that there is no kitchen help. Marie shakes her head and removes the tea table. Carlota stops her long enough to recover the newspaper, which she places on one of the side tables.)

You've not said much about yourself. I understand
you're overwhelmed, and not a little frightened.
I know you must have a thousand questions.
Go play the D-flat Prelude while I change
(Yes, the one they call "The Raindrop."). I asked
Marie to bring me — where? —

(Marie points her to a folding screen. Carlota vanishes behind it. The sound of the visitor tentatively touching the piano keys is heard, and then the Chopin "D-Flat Prelude" is played.)

the gown I wore when I first disembarked
that midnight we landed in Veracruz.

(Emerges from behind the screen wearing an old crinoline dress. It is dusty, and cobwebs trail from it. She moves in time with the music, stately, regal. The speech in the following lines slows to the pace of the music.)

A broad and billowing crinoline dress,
like this — forgive the cobwebs everywhere!—
and over it — ah, *there*, Marie — that shawl

(Marie brings the shawl, and places it over Carlota's shoulders.)

the modest ladies' shawl, the *rehozzo*.
In Mexico, décolleté is art,
a sudden, unexpected blossoming
when the shawl parts, so! and a well-placed fan

(reaches without looking and finds her fan, then opens it with a flourish)

directs the gaze of but a single man
(or one who thinks he is the only man). —
Oh! what I learned from mestizo women!

How did we wear our hair in those days? You,
my dear, are so discreetly coiffed, not like
those flappers one sees in *Le Monde's* gravure,
so you would appreciate our fashions.
My hair – thank you, it's as black as ever —

(Marie makes a gesture indicating that Carlota is deluded, but Carlota sees it.)

Don't contradict me, Marie — how dare you!
(The insolence of servants!) My — black — hair
was done in Mailand fashion, I kept these —

(She goes into a drawer in the side table and finds her hair attachment.)

Do keep on playing, my ear, it's lovely! —
They just attach, you see, these hanging knots
on either ear, the grapevines of Bacchus,
heavy enough to induce a migraine!
Still, very flattering. My mirror, Marie!

(Marie goes to the dresser to find a hand-mirror.)

I want to remember that moment
when the ships fired their guns in our honor,

(Takes the mirror from Marie)
how I looked then, when Max and I touched land,
solid ground after weeks of sailing and storms.

(Holds up the mirror and looks at herself)

    (Almost a scream) MON DIEU, NON!
    (The music stops abruptly, mid-note)
                                         Even in this light, a hag!
I am so old! I am — so — old! So — old.

(Her hand falls away with the mirror, and Marie rushes to catch it as it falls from her hand).

Let me sit! Take these dreadful things away! *(Two beats)*
Who is that sitting at the piano?
Show me your face! *You!* Oh yes, you, my dear,
you were playing me the "Raindrop" Prelude
and I was back in Eighteen Sixty-four!

Sixty years now since I left Mexico!
I was your age! Yours! *(A beat)* Why did I not die?
Why do this house and I keep lingering?

(Carlota slumps forward, near collapse).
Why? .... Why? .... Why?

(Marie persuades her to give up the mirror, and guides her back to her chair. Carlota, weeping, seems distracted, even unsure where she is. Then she notices the "Mailand" hair attachments and removes them, waving Marie to come and take them from her. At this moment their roles are reversed, and Marie is clearly nurse/mother to her feeble charge. Marie indicates with a gesture, joined hands against her cheek, that Carlota should take a nap.)

I am not tired, Marie. I shall not sleep!
I am still here for Max, as ... are ... we ... all!
I have so much to do! Arms to purchase.
Cannons to fit in the gunboats. Supplies
for the army — all those young men to feed.
Belgium will come to the aid of Mexico!
When was a woman ever asked for more?
I am all Max has. Hand him to me!

(Marie produces the Max doll from behind the empty chair next to Carlota. It is almost marionette-size, a bright officers' uniform with epaulets. Several of the limbs have been replaced with tree twigs and branchlets. Instead of a doll's head there is an animal skull, and a kind of wig made from straw atop it.)

Marie, his hair's askew! He doesn't have
a twig of a finger on his left hand!
Go out and find his comb, and the blue cape
he likes to put on when it's winter here.

(Marie goes to a small dresser, opens a drawer, and searches.)

Come, look, my child! It's only a rag-thing.
For years I had a proper soldier doll.
It even had a Habsburg beard like Max.

(Speaking to the visitor in a lower voice, in confidence)

But *one* no longer connected, or soon
to be no longer connected with me,
one took it, when the influenza came,
took it and *burned it* while I fevered on.

I saw her do it — I watched with that toy, *(pointing to the window)*,
my own little periscopic spyglass.

(Servants!) *(Looking back, she sees Marie leaving the stage with the tea table.)*

Just as there's *one* who substitutes
paste for my authentic diamonds.
Diamonds I need to raise an armada!
(Raises her voice so that Marie can hear)
I once had forty ladies-in-waiting! Forty!
And look at what I am left with now!

But Max Eternal is not to be stopped
by some spiteful bonfire in the courtyard.
I made another from some twisted cloth,
a dog's head with a wig made of straw,
glass eyes I plucked from an old stuffed owl —
and branches make passable arms and legs.
A little witchcraft softens madness, *n'est-ce pas?*

(She holds up the doll for her visitor's inspection, then places it gently on the seat beside her.)

You know it was Napoleon the Third
who put us on the Mexican throne,
he and a handful of the landowners.
Bankers and profiteers behind it all.
They told us there had been a plebiscite,
that the Mexican people had begged us
to come and be their monarchs. All lies! Lies!
We were so foolish and young, Max and I.
We came into Veracruz port by night.
The people didn't come to welcome us.
It was late. All the garden gates were closed,
the walled streets as silent as a graveyard.
How the cathedral loomed in the moonlight!
And then I saw what was watching us, and shrieked:
vultures on the roof — vultures on the cross,
dancing like crippled Jesuits in the plaza —

there is a way they turn their wings inward *(gestures)*
and waddle obscenely to some dead thing.
"Why don't you kill them?" I implored.
"Your majesty," someone explained to me,
"Those are *zopilotes,* zo—pi—lo—tes.
Always they are here. Without the vultures,
Who would clean the streets?"
                                          I should have seen it
for the bad omen it certainly was.
Our thrones were propped on a French invasion.
The Juarez government, the elected
and proper government had fled up north.
Our royal palace was inhabited
by rats and vermin. I can tell it now —
it seems almost amusing to me now —
The Mexican Emperor and Empress
spent their first night — on a billiard table.
We took the old hall of Chalpultepec,
and how the old landowners flocked to see.
We gave balls and banquets and operas.
Max built his new pleasure gardens, just like
the ones we had fashioned at Miramar.
We actually grew to love the Mexicans,
but the hearts of the poor people were crushed
by poverty and the rapacious church.

(She picks up Max and puts him on her lap)

It's all right, Max, we may now speak of it —
to whom could anyone betray us now?

And all the while we breathed the mango air
and I loved the capital more and more.
Rome wanted back the lands and privileges
they had from the bloody hands of Cortez.
The landowners were just as rapacious.
And the priests! They left the dead unburied
if the poor could not make an offering.
Gold to marry, gold to baptize, more gold
to put your mother into a coffin.

Max knew a wise king could settle these things.
We sent the Pope's reptilian
agent back to Rome. We gave them nothing!
Max would have handed the government
to Juarez. "Be my prime minister," he said!
But Juarez played cat and mouse from the north.
The "elected president" with his armies,
baiting the French into futile battles —
wearing us down, month after weary month,
a land so huge we could hardly map it!
Juarez, that implacable Indian —
he never stopped. He never stopped.

(Marie arrives with the tea refreshed, and some pastries on the platter. Carlota permits Marie to move Max to his seat).

My dear, I'm boring you with politics.
It's not supposed to be a woman's work.
They say we do not care — don't we care *more*,
we who become the widows of dreamers?

There's still tea if you can stand it. I can't
be sure these pastries have all been tasted.
Yes, Max, I hear you. There's no one living
who'd want to poison me now. That lecher
Napoleon the Third is gone — Habsburgs,
one and all — the Hohenzollerns — even
the Romanovs, Nicholas, Alexei,
the Tsarina and all her fine daughters.
How have we lived to see these awful things?
Only you and I, Max, have outlived them.

They don't speak much about Maximilian.
How brave he was when the French deserted
us, he and his few Mexican generals.
Then they captured Max at Querétaro,
a desert place, a walled fort, terrible.

I was in Europe, beleaguering kings
to rescue our tottering new Empire.
Napoleon would not dare call on me:

I stormed his bedchamber and made a scene.
There he lay, doubled in pain, a monster,
lord of France, a lecher on a bedpan.
Master of thirty mistresses, they said.
Even his diseases had infections.
He had become a bloated thing, doubled
upon himself in exquisite pain. Louis,
the Emperor of France, *sa Majesté*.
His curse — did you know? — *he could not piss.*

He babbled about Bismarck and Germany,
how no more ships would go to Mexico.
"You fool," he snapped at me. "Why isn't Max
here with you now? The empire is over."

I went to see Piu Nino in Rome. The Pope himself.
Pope Pius the Ninth could not refuse me! Me!
His hand blessed our going to Mexico.
I denounced the old creature to his face.
He reeked of cigars and brandy. I kissed
his ring and rose like an eagle, grabbed hold
of his hand and wouldn't let go of it.
"Keep your word!" I told him. "Keep Mexico
for the monarchs you sent to protect it!"

(Two beats.)
A toad would have given me more comfort.

What could I do? I, an Empress in flight.
My escort, my servants, my entourage:
each day their number diminished. Behind
my back they whispered, plotted, betrayed me.
What would I have have done without my Marie?
I was followed everywhere. French agents,
Jesuits, even a nun with poisoned bread.
I fell down shrieking in the Vatican.

I don't remember coming here to Meysse.
There were doctors everywhere and nuns
(kind ones, not like those toothless poisoners).
Did my father ever come here, Marie? *(Marie shakes her head)*

<268>

There were months of fever and too much sleep.
I had no letters. They wouldn't tell me
Juarez had ordered Maximilian shot.
Even Americans begged them not to,
but they killed him, with his two generals.
Hand me the portfolio, please, Marie —
I promise not to be upset. Show her.

(Marie displays a portfolio to the visitor or audience – a print of Maximilian's execution).

This was engraved in Mexico — they fired
from so close up. It looks like him, of course.
He forgave the soldiers. They played their role,
he his. He cried out "Long live Mexico!"

(Sound of a gunfire is heard. Carlota covers her ears, but Marie does not hear it.)

Manet has painted the scene, so I am told,
but that would be as he imagined it.

Thank God the *real* Max is here beside me.
He is not that thing that fell in the sand.
He is not that one-eyed mummy they made
and shipped in a glass box to Trieste.
This is Max, Emperor of Mexico,
Max is now *Emperor of Everything.*
Did you know I am a king's grand-daughter?
Louis-Philippe of France, usurped by lechers.
And I am a king's daughter — Leopold
of Belgium. Belgium the damp and moldy.
I have not tasted a mango for years!

See now why Berlioz should make my opera:
Aeneas leaves Dido, Carlota leaves Max.
One flees, one dies, oh, what an opera!

(Laughs, then looks off into space as though she were seeing the curtain rising on her own story.)

Have you been to the Opera, my young friend?
Faust and *Figaro*, *Figaro* and *Faust*,
isn't it tiresome? But my own opera *(a beat, looks off into space, shrugs)*
what would it all be for? And who would care?

I suppose it should all have a moral.
If you would seek advice from Carlota
who has lived life bitter and true, it's this:
To love once, and never abdicate that love.
To find your home and never surrender it.
To trust no judgment better than your own.

We come to our own if we only wait.
They say I am mad — I am gladly so.
They say that Max is dead — I say he's not.
He sits beside me here. We hear guitars
at sunset. Sometimes they serenade us
with "*Adios Mama Carlota,*" that
song that followed me on to Veracruz
when I went back alone to Europe. I
know the song was mocking me. *Adios* —
they knew I would never return again —
but hearing it still makes me cry —.

(The song, "Adiós, Mamá Carlota," for voice and guitar, is heard offstage. The song is interrupted by the ringing of a church bell. It tolls five times. Maria appears with the Guest's coat over her arm).

                                                         Those bells!
Ah, those bells! — those will be the vespers now.
That means our visit is nearly over.
I would walk you out to the garden gate,
but darkness comes, and the black vultures
start gathering upon the roofs and walls.
They followed me from Veracruz, you know.
They hover, and light, and huddle and strut.
They must have nested — each spring there are more.

(She goes to window and raises her spyglass-periscope).

Ah, there they are, already. The vultures!
Maybe they know another war is due.

(She turns her back to the audience)

Zopilotes for me ...
                    zopilotes for Max...
                                      poor, poor Mexico!

THE PRISONER: A ONE-SCENE VERSE PLAY

Setting: An Austrian police station in the first decade of the 19th century. A heavily-barred door with a small peephole. A trapdoor in mid-stage revealing a stairwell down into prison cells. Dim, flickering torchlight from below. A table with two chairs, with light enough to read provided by a high window on the far wall.

Characters: Kommandant KLEIBER
Lieutenant KRAUS
Voice of Prisoner

KLEIBER (*pounding outside the massive front door, which has been barred from the inside*)
What do you mean, "Who goes there?" Idiot!
Unbar this door at once and let me in!

KRAUS (*peeking through the narrow window in the door, then hastily unbarring it*)
Ah, mein Kommandant! You needn't have come!

KLEIBER (*pulling a handful of papers from his overcoat.*)
Such shouting, Kraus! I've never heard the like.
My guests are beside themselves with worry.
Have you got some madman here in the cells?
And what is this? (*shaking paper in Kleiber's face*)
    What do you mean by this?
Sending notes to Vienna without my orders!

PRISONER (*A baritone voice, almost bellowing, calls from below:*)
Release me! This room isn't fit for swineherds!
Get back, you pig-headed ruffians! (*A crash*) Ah!

KRAUS
We can't keep him quiet, mein Kommandant.
You needn't have interrupted your evening.

KLEIBER
An ordinary madman. Laudanum
is all we should need to quiet him down.
Why hasn't Doctor Schmitt been sent for? Schmitt,
damn you, not the Inspector General?
 (*waves papers again*)

KRAUS (*obsequiously helping Kleiber remove his coat*)
This is no madman, Kommandant.

PRISONER (*shouting*)
                              Morons!

KRAUS
Oh, he's a clever one. A spy, I say.
We'll all get promotions for catching him.

KLEIBER (*moving to the back of the table, sitting down, while Kraus brushes off the Kommandant's coat and hangs it up*)
We won't get a pig's eyelash, Kraus. Spies? Here?
In fact, you may get demoted for this.
What's here to snoop out but a beer garden,
two churches, some broken-down vineyards?

KRAUS (*rolls his eyes at his superior's ignorance, sits in the other chair, and leans forward*)
When trouble comes, it follows the water.
And what do we have right here? (*pointing out the window*).
 The canal!
The canal runs right to the capital.
The French could be coming, Bonaparte —

KLEIBER (*crossing himself*)
                              Don't
ever say "Bonaparte" in here! That bastard!
That traitor to all that is right and good!

<273>

KRAUS
If not the French, we have the Russians, too.
Those bushy-bearded Patriarchs, and that
crooked cross they worship, ready to leap
and add us to the Romanoff dung-heap.

KLEIBER
You're very up on politics. Next thing
you'll be saying the madman's a Turk!

PRISONER
I demand to speak to the governor
of this filthy, degrading prison. Back!
Don't come near me with that! Damn you! Damn you!
(Another crash)

KLEIBER *(walking to trap door entrance, lifting it)*
Men! Quiet down there! Don't annoy the man!

KRAUS *(as Kleiber resumes his seat)*
He *is* as dark as a Turk. And his clothes!
The tavern woman refused to serve him.
"Geschmutzig!" she called him. "Mudboot! Sootcollar!"
They're right: you can really smell him. Go down
and take a whiff and let it call itself
an artist and a gentleman!

KLEIBER
      Gypsies
and Jews and riffraff. No inn will serve them.
If they but turned him out, he would have walked.
We'd be none the wiser. One beggar less,
he'd be in someone else's jail by now.

KRAUS
Well, they served him. Dinner he demanded,
the best Liebfraumilch from out our vineyards.
Two bottles down, a chicken, six sausages,
and then he comes up with "Ah! No money!"
That's when the shouting started, and the fight.
He hadn't a kroner on him. "Florins,"

he said, "I have florins." His pockets out,
nothing in there but lint and a pen-knife.
Then all his bag went tug-of-war: out flew
notebooks, some chewed-up carpenter's pencils,
but not a single copper coin — not one.

KLEIBER
Nothing you've told me, not ... one ... Thing, Herr Kraus,
is out of the ordinary. This is no spy,
just some specimen of human flotsam.

PRISONER *(begins humming and singing, wordless, disjointed, the notes a monotone, with strong syncopated accents, then)*

KRAUS
The singing is worse yet than the cursing!

KLEIBER *(lifting his hand)*
Wait! Wait! I think I — *(the prisoner's singing abruptly stops. Kleiber shakes his head, turns his attention back to Kraus)*

KRAUS
I had my eye on him all day, you see.
He had a method. A method, indeed.
He'd sit, he'd open this little notebook,
   (pulls notebook from drawer in table)
pretending to watch birds, admire the view,
oh, really clever he was about it.
A little he'd sing *(imitates the prisoner's monotone)*,
   then lick the pencil, so *(imitates gesture)*
then make some marks. Then on he went some more.
Another good spot he'd find, and *(sings monotones)*
   and *(does licking gesture)*
He was ... *drawing the canal* ... you see?
   (waves the notebook).

KLEIBER *(beginning to take Kraus seriously)*
You saw all this? You watched him, unobserved?

KRAUS
I saw everything. He counted his steps,
tapped one hand on another, eyes flashing
so machine-like and mathematical,
numbers and measures all down in these marks.
To the naïve eye there's nothing in here
but lines, and crosses, and smudges; to me
it's all a code. A *code*, mein Kommandant,
and where there are codes, there are enemies!
(Opens the book and puts it between them)

PRISONER *(in a normal tone)*
I need light. Could I at least have a candle?
And a pen and paper? Does that mean "No?"
Do you chinless burgers speak any language?

KRAUS
These vertical lines — see how he's *counting*.
He's marking all our fortifications.
This way the invaders will know our town,
the little streams, the vineyard boundaries.
Their cannons *(pointing) here* will knock our steeples down.
He put up quite a roar when we took this.

KLEIBER *(searches his pocket for his eyeglasses)*
And how did he account for himself, then?

KRAUS
He says he *walked* from Vienna. Leagues off!
He says he is "given to Nature walks."

KLEIBER *(cleaning off his glasses)*
As are Goethe and a lot of Germans.

KRAUS
He was filthy, I tell you. A collar
that hadn't seen laundry since 1800.
His coat a ragged patchwork, and his shoes,
well, one was so unlike the other, you'd
think he'd robbed a battlefield for wardrobe.

He wanted a night coach back to Vienna.
He dared to say he knows the Emperor.
Imagine that getup at court! It's clear
he's a suspicious character. That's why
I wrote the message at once

KLEIBER
       I know, Kraus.
(As though quoting) "By Our Imperial Order, Round Up.
Interrogate. Then Escort to Prison."

KRAUS *(confidently)*
Who knows just what we may have caught ourselves?
On this one day, our fortunes might be made.
If I can only crack this code of his,
it's *von Kraus* for me, *von Kleiber* for you.

KLEIBER
Don't get ahead of yourself. You've not left
this village, you know. And I spent two years
at University. I know Latin.
Just let me see that notebook now.
(with an imperious gesture, adjusts his glasses and regards the book)

KRAUS *(impatient, pointing)*
Here, Kommandant. These parallel lines, see?
Crosses and smudges and little arrows.
It's almost certainly an invasion plan.

KLEIBER
You've got it turned sideways, Kraus. Idiot!
Those lines aren't vertical. Those smudges — *ah!* —
Those crosses! Those "little arrows." *Mein Gott!*
(jumps up, letting his chair fall back the floor, runs to the trap door and opens it)
Mein Gott! Downstairs now! To the cells! Down, man!
(pushes Kraus ahead of him)

KRAUS *(Descending below-stage)*
What is it Kommandant? Shall we send word to Vienna immediately?

KLEIBER *(Following him. The remaining lines all spoken from below stage, with lights flashing and sounds of feet pounding down stairs)*
Quiet! Follow me. Follow me. A light, there!
Brighter! Let me see! What have you done?
You fool! You have arrested BEETHOVEN!

SYMPHONIE FANTASTIQUE

SYMPHONIE FANTASTIQUE

After the Symphony by Hector Berlioz

1
First Movement: Dreams, Passions
I did not plan this passion.
Your voice intruded on my consciousness,
its foreign lilt, its strange inflections,
the way your meter'd tongue dropped pearls
of Shakespeare, Poe and Baudelaire,
the way your eyes implored me
as though it were my destiny
to grapple with some hooded Darkness
to win you for myself.

But what am I?
What is my frail embrace
to beauty such as yours?
All eyes are chained to you.
See how the students crave your neck,
the soldiers admire your slender waist,
the old men yearn for your kisses —
an army would not suffice for you!
I am your unknown conqueror.
I am the one who sends you violets,
a myrtle wreath, a sonnet.

Others impress you with jewelry,
offer to garb you in silk and velvet.
I stood at the fringe of the stage door crowd.
Strong ones pressed in toward you —
oh, the broad-shouldered ones,
the lion's-mane heroes, the uniforms!
I was the shadow at the edge of gas lamp.
You smiled, touched hands,
absorbing their love like a thirsty plant,
rose blush rising on your ivory cheek.
You never noticed me —
not tonight, nor on all the other nights.

But then my heart rose up
a double timpani of triumph.
You entered your carriage,
one hand enfolding a *billet doux*
(still in its envelope, unread perhaps),
the other protecting a fragile bouquet —

my violets! my violets! oh god,
tonight you will read my poems,
tonight you will know that I love you!

I walk the streets all night,
chilled by the Seine
on half a dozen crossings.
I pause before the gray cathedral,
look up into the knowing clouds
that hurtle eastward
to the sunrise.
The rosette window is dark,
for all the candles
and their attendant prayers
have guttered out.
This night *my* angel,
    good or ill,
is absent. I am resigned.
The heavens will do nothing.
My words alone shall win you.

iii
Third Movement: Scene in the Fields
You shepherds, play!
You know not what your fluted night
    does to the haunted.
You wind, rising in harmony,
I think you plowed great ships
    across some sea,
you tasted salt not of tears only.
Look how you grapple
  with the landlocked cedars,
  birch staffs taut as ropes,
  leaf sails tattering.

The trees snap back, you drown
   the frail reed pipes
   and rage with your own voice
   among the mountain pines.

The shepherds flee. Now double thunder
rolls from peak to valley,
a mournful rumbling
of discontent, as though the gods
had lovers just as oblivious
as she to me.

If these vast and terrible beings
can gain no solace, then what of me?

Would I were dead and gone, would that
bare earth and unabating wind
outlived me, sole dwellers
of an everlasting night!

If I were left
to wolf and vulture,
to eagle, crow and carrion —
if only these pages
   (made orchestral by a hand
   unseen that guides my hand!)
remained, spun down
to the valley, the river, the sea.

If one day decades hence,
   this poem falls from an opened book
into your startled view, or,
passing the concert hall
you hear the corresponding melodies
and discern your name in them,

would you recall me then,
    knowing the one who loved you
    left a bleached skull
    on a granite mountain
    a heartbeat petrified
    into a stony silence
    the thunder punctuates?

My solitary end is pointless
    unless its iron-black pole
can draw you to it.
I will live on, and draw new breath;
I will return to you, unwelcome
as my love has been, not loving,
but as the Messenger of Death.
The pale throat I love,
    I will crush beneath my hands.

Op 16/183 1963/1967/1979/2011

KEZIAH MASON

After H.P. Lovecraft's "Dreams in the Witch House" (1932)

"Something's not right
   about Keziah,"
the midwife tells
   the scholar father,
   Pastor Mason,
the Salem Divine.
The doting mother
won't hear of it.
"Bad auspices," the father nods.
"I told you so."

The mother cradles it
   as midwife scurries off
with rags and the bloody
   umbilical,
an accusing serpent.
"Baby Keziah," the mother croons,
"my perfect child."

"Not right, bad auspices,
   bad numerology,
too many vowels,
bad luck to have alpha
   follow zed that way."

She waves him away.
Anxious, he follows
   the weary midwife,
   Old Goodie Brown.
Their eyes meet.
"Tell me, " he asks.
"Why didn't you say
if I have a son or daughter?"

"Neither," she says.
"Who knows," she shrugs,
"what it will grow to?"

"Deformed?" he guesses.
She shakes her head.
"Hermaphrodite?"
Her eyes avoid him.
"The ancients write
of such creatures."

The midwife hesitates,
taking the small purse
he discreetly offers.
"I've seen odd things,
good Pastor Mason,
but never this:
not male, not female.
What's there,
I'd call *machinery*,
and what use God
or the Devil intends for it
I'll not be thinking on."

She hurries out
into the snowstorm,
the bloodied rag
held tight,
not one but *two*
umbilicals,
a black-furred thing
    whose razor teeth
gnaw and consume
    the after-birth.

"There, there," she coos,
    petting its fur,
as a tiny facsimile
of the Pastor's face
stares up at her.
"Old Goodie Brown
    will look out
for her little Jenkin,
my perfect child."

Then the thing cleared
its tiny throat
and after a dry
and preliminary chittering
it thanked her
in fourteen languages.

KEZIAH'S GEOMETRY LESSONS

"Something's not right
    about Keziah."
So spoke the tutor
old Mason,
    the defrocked minister
hired for his
    only daughter's lessons
in Latin and Greek,
    geometry and music.

The old man sighed.
    Five tutors had fled
    at the sight of his hideous daughter.
    This one had stayed
    three months — the record.
She labored him, not he, her,
in Latin; her Greek,
    the tutor felt,
was somehow pre-Homeric,
littered with words not in
his Hellenic lexicon.

"Is it the Greek again?
    She's stubborn."
The tutor — his name was William —
waved his thin hand,
    which seemed thinner
    if that was possible,
    than when he arrived.
(He had been eating
    noticeably less at table
    since moving his lodgings
    to the upper garret).

"No, the geometry.
   The things she says,
although she knows her Euclid,
are troubling me. She draws,
first squares, then cubes,
then hints at something
   unrepresentable —
      a cube cubed
      or transcended,
each of its six facets
   exploded
to fifty-four invisible forms —
yet only visible, *she* says
   by *standing outside
and seeing from above.*
   'The cube I draw,'
she tells me
   'is but a mouse-hole
   to the higher space.
   Can ye not see there?' "

"Is she mad,
   do you think,
or a kind of genius?"
the father muses.

"She lacks constraint,"
the tutor speculates.
"It's not the way
a young woman thinks."
He pauses.
"Or a Christian."

"Indulge her,"
old Mason tells him,
"for neither cross
nor catechism
can come near her.
She will not leave this house
till I can marry her
to some doddering scholar

or ship captain derelict,
someone who will find her
amusing, her dowry
adequate, so long
as he expects no peace —
    or children."

The tutor gleans
at last, some sense
of Mason's burden, the why
of his abandonment
of Bible and congregants.
Keziah was God's
affliction for his own
pride of intellect,
a strident mind
in a hunch-dwarf body,
his penance
to be her keeper.

The tutor withdrew,
prepared for bed,
washed himself everywhere,
lay naked
the better to attract
his guilty pleasure,
his imaginary lover
by whose graces
he no longer need commit
the sin of self-pollution,

to await *its* coming,
to please *its* inquisitive,
    pulsating and thrusting
    machinery,
when it arrived,
    not through the door
        or window,
but from the crazed-angle corner
    he filled with plaster
        to unsquare it

and through whose polyhedrous
    mouse hole
it came
    a congeries of bubble-forms
    to a geometer
as fair as Helen
    before even Menelaus
    took her, let alone
    Trojan Paris,

with whom he flew
    rhapsode ecstatic,
feeding and fed upon,
sung to and singing,

his Bible too,
unopened for weeks now,
turned down in the corner;
April's end his own end
as she witch-waltzes
him to a Greek Walpurgis
he neither expects
nor wishes to survive.

His climax-death
will span eons and galaxies,
feelers and tentacles a-quiver,
hydrofluoric neurons
    in orgasmic tremor,
worlds colliding, orbits
    asunder, seismic,
ichthyc, arachnid,
    reptilian pleasuring.

Keziah likes him.
And whom Keziah loves,
she shares with her gods.

TRUE FRIENDS

For Pierre and Jen

True friends
are those who downplay
your protestations
of seasonal depression,
drawing you out
on the shunned holiday
and its grim barrage
of hurled presents,

who ply you with roast beef
and good cheer;
good talk, too,
of all our friends
who are sliding to their ruin
save thee and me;

who, gleaning your thoughts
as moonlight glistens
on nearby snow mounds,
propose a midnight walk
through a densely-peopled place
where not one voice is caroling,
not one wine drunk reels,
and dead trees worthy
of Caspar David Friedrich
thrust vine-clogged branch
into the lunar orb's
eye-socket: a tramp
to the glazed and silent pond
of the North Burial Ground.

If there be Yule or Wassail,
raise cups
at Nicholas Brown's
bilingual obelisk,
the Latin side well-lit
for night-bird reading,

or tip your cap
to the derelict women's
Last Home on Earth
(the potter's field
of the workhouse), or heave
the old year's slave-chains
into the mailbox vault
of John Brown's shattered
table-top tombstone.

Too chill for even
the flitter of bat,
the night is warm despite,
the august society
of graveyard walkers
our aristocracy.

AUTUMN ON PLUTO

Charon has set
   below the Plutonian horizon.
Beneath the dimmer satellites,
   desolate Nix and even dimmer Hydra,
an autumn tree of volcanic glass
   glints like a spiderweb, leaf-cups
athirst for lunar light, weak beams
   more doubt than promise,

orbs almost black in total blackness,
real only in those eye-blinks
when they occlude some distant star.

Blue-black obsidian limbs
   cascade to branchlets,
death-willow leaflets serrated and thin,
   not falling (as there is no wind
      here ever) but *flung*
with crossbow efficiency,
   a flight of tri-lobed arrows
sharper than surgical knives.

The only red of this world's autumn
   is blood-flow as deer
(the stock and store of Hades)
   collapse in agony,
and silicon roots thrust funnel
   and thirsty filament
to drink from the spreading rust
of severed carotids,
pierced hearts pumping,
antler and bone and hide
a-pile the slaughter-field.

After a few weeks' wintering,
    the branchlets crackle and split
as red-berry buds form perfect spheres,
Pluto's cornelian cherries,
untouched, inedible
amid the bone and gemstone clutter
    of dead Arcady.

Not far from Acheron's turgid flow
(nitrous ice in a methane river),
dread Hades dreams of venison,
afloat in sauce of cornelian cherry.
Persephone wipes clean
    his fevered brow, proffers
a bowl of wheat-porridge
    and raisins, the flesh
of olive and apricot. He sighs.
She can only make
    what her mother Ceres taught her.
The juice of venison has never
    run down her chin, nor has
she savored the sourest of cherries
drowned in bee-honey.

He must count the days
    till her vernal journey upward,
till he can pluck the victims
from beneath the kill-deer willow,
fill baskets with precious cornel fruit,
then call forth poets and heroes
    (Hephaestus and Mars as well
    if he's in a generous spirit),
for a bone-gnaw feast
around the lava pit,
a bard-and-boast orgy
of odes and war-talk.

It goes on for weeks, and
although the words they speak
are apt to freeze between one's mouth
and the receiving ear,
for the summer-widower Hades,
death is a bowl of cherries.

DAWN

He thinks: if someone could describe this scene,
it would be stark and simple, a blond-haired man
leans forward on a folding chair. The air is chill,
though no breath rises from his nose or mouth.
He is quite still, as nightbird songs beyond
the French windows subside to that hush
that precedes the dawn, the guard change
from nightingale to lark. To him,
the room appears to be empty. Although he feels
cold steel through his tight, black jeans
and the damp tug of the back of his T-shirt
to the seat-back, he cannot see himself.
His clothes are likewise invisible to him.

He can feel the breath in his nostrils, press lips
against the back of his hand to prove he is there.
His vision, sharp as an owl's, sees all
that passes on the lawn and garden,
down to the tiniest roil of mouse and vole,
but he is blind to his own hand before his face.

Anyone entering the room would see him.
He supposedly looks awfully good for his years,
three hundred to the day if his memory serves him.
This English house has endured much: riots and war,
Zeppelin and V-2 attacks, the onslaught of blight
and public housing. His well-paid agents
have kept the house intact, managed his gold
with great discretion, and shielded his name
from prying scholars and historians. A blind wall
of trust funds secure his quotidian (quotinoctian?)
needs and secures the multiple vaults, some linked
to one another by passages no rat could fathom.

He has been the perfect vampire, discreet
in his comings and goings as a Windsor heir,
and London's finest have never discerned him
as a creature of great need and urgency:
a city envelops and forgets so many deaths.

His very contentment, the ease with which
he goes about his business, is the very cause
of his decision to end it — his life — or whatever
this existence is called — at the three-century mark.
He will let the sunlight do it: he waits for dawn
by the eastern doorway, the old drapes
and their dustwebs pulled to the floor, the lace
of even older curtains torn to tatters, panes
broken to admit the acid beams of daylight.

And after this? He assumes: oblivion.
The vampire life did not come with a manual.
The already undead are all clueless; for all
he knows the universe was just one vast
hunger for blood, the feeding and being fed,
the *summa* as well as the *sine qua non*.

Just one thing has him curious:
It is said that a vampire, on dying,
can see his own reflection then,
and at no other time in his undead
existence. All the more poignant,
that he has assembled all the mirrors
this decrepit house possesses:
two sets of dresser triptychs; a pile
of hand mirrors and shaving glasses
(the vanity of guests and how much fun
to creep up on them as they regard themselves
in all-too-flattering lamplight!);
three full-length wall mirrors leaned
    against chair-backs.

Mirror upon mirror, until the gaze dizzies
in endless fun house angles,
an infinity of floor tiles, chair legs
    and angled corners, eye-twinkle
of the six-armed candelabra
into constellations of ever-diminishing stars,
a kaleidoscope of everything there is,
but not a glimmer of him.

What will they find, afterwards,
if they track his most careless, audacious
killing to this house at last,
or when they come some day to demolish it?
The dust or whatever it is that he leaves behind
like a spilled hourglass? Or just the empty room
with its puzzlement of mirrors, that wide bed
canopied with cobwebs, whose dark sheets conceal
untold congelations of victims' blood?

They will find the clothes, of course:
a closet full of black suits, black jeans,
black leather jackets, black Calvin Klein
dress shirts and T's, all fitting his mode
of "fashion model gone Goth boy."
Yes, too, there's a black opera cape,
wolf-fur trimmed with red velvet lining,
black shoes in every style since 1780
(strange how they never seem to wear out)
right up to present-day sneakers, all black,
black gloves and a variety of useful luggage,
leather, black. Odd that he can only see them
as they hang in the closet: one slip of hand
into a glove or jacket, one toe inside
a shoe or pantleg, and it vanishes, gone
to his own eyes and to the mirror.

How strange to be real only to others,
to touch a willing neck or shoulders
yet never see your hand doing it, never to sense
except by touch his nose-end, toe or fingertip.
How long it took to become at ease and graceful,
even — to see a wineglass rise magically
before one's one eyes and come to lips,
and then on top of that to have to feign
drinking, to let a wine-wash cross his palette
then fall discreetly back into the glass: that took
a lot of practice! At least the clothes were simpler
now: no more the Edwardian dandy, he slid
into a T-shirt and pulled on jeans as fast
as any teenager. One merely had to remember
zippers and not be inside-out or backwards.

This could have gone on forever, of course,
but the people have grown less interesting,
more easily fooled, more of them glazed
stupid drunk or reeling from drug to drug,
others were smug oxen, waiting the day
their personal savior delivered them.
Who knew it would come, the night
when he could walk into a Goth bar,
and announce "I am a vampire" and silence
followed? A trio of black-clad women
flash plastic vampire teeth and smile,
ask which coven he belongs to.
He discerns two types: the overdressed
in opera garb — though none, from their dull
look had even been to an opera — and the
down-dressed in some kind of torn rags
punctuated with metal grommets. The men
in both groups eye and dismiss him.
No uniform, no admission, it seems.

He lingers a while over a red drink
he does not even feign to taste, his ears
offended by machine noise attempting
to form itself into music. A young man
in the torn pin-cushion mode comes up,

makes sure he sees the Old English lettering
on his T-shirt that reads, VAMPIRE VICTIM.
"You're new," the young man says.
He nods. "You're the real thing, aren't you?"
He nods. "Will you kill me?"
He nods. He's happy to oblige, but bored.

There was something to be said for the struggle.
The hunt, and its danger, and the threat
of discovery had been The Great Game for him.
He liked it best when they resisted. Sometimes
he almost let them win, or even escape
in order to overtake and surprise them later.
There was a moment, always, the pause
when he pulled from a throat in drinking
and looked the victim eye-to-eye, a dark
and terrible secret that nature withholds:

the victim in that moment loves the killer,
admires his superior essence, gives up
his life force in abject adoration.
Every one of them said "Kill me,"
if not in words then in eyes' surrender.

What he could never know, was what they saw:
whatever was in their eyes, was not him.

He takes the boy by the scruff of the neck,
and passing the bar he reaches deftly
for three crystal sherry glasses, cupped
between the fingers of his left hand.

The club, which billed itself Tartarus,
(the place beneath Hell if one needed explaining),
had, as clubs are wont, an alleyway out back,
trash cans and strident ailanthus trees, dark spots
behind high shrubbery against a chain link fence.

Right hand against the boy's chest, he feels
the terrified and excited heartbeat rise
as neck veins flush to readiness, oh, too easy!
He rends the shirt away, leans down, parts flesh
with his expert incisors, inhales the blood
like a breath of fresh air, takes it in fast,
faster than he has done for years, the breath
fails, the heart falters — no! he pulls back,
pounds at the ribcage to start the heart again —
he would not be cheated – the boy's mouth
is frozen in an *oh!* of horror and *No, I
didn't really want this won't you please stop?*

He doesn't stop — he ends the life that bleeds
beneath him, sucks dry the husk of heat,
life and the great force that animates all things
like a great and overflowing battery.
This ought to be exciting, yet in a moment
he is sated, this death as boring
as a fast-food hamburger. What to do
with the body? With strength he knew
no way to measure he lifts the limp form
and shakes it against the steel grid of fence,
firm, then fast, then faster, till bone and tendon,
flesh and skull and garment all pass on through
like cabbage through a grater,

soft wet fragments falling through, as cloth
slides down, a heap of belt and pants and grommets.
This was not his usual, careful feeding. The mess
would be considerable, the mystery
of how a man passed through chain links
a riddle for the local police station.

Dogs were coming; he sensed them already,
a feral pack that followed him everywhere
and often helped him in the aftermath.
With luck, they would drag off the bones
and fragments: no matter anyway,
since this would be his last feeding.
Re-entering the Goth club, quite unaware

of whether his T-shirt is dark with heart-blood
he approaches the trio of vampirellas
and puts down, with perfect balance,
three brimful sherry glasses, still warm
with the victim's body heat. "On the house,"
he tells them. "Drink — if you dare."
He smiles his best smile, puts hand to lips
and makes a downward, smearing motion
in hopes they will see blood there.
They stare at him, then at the glasses.
He is at the door; he is out. No one
has said a word or moved to stop him.
He hands a hundred to the bouncer, who nods
an assurance of his forgetting his ever
having been there, turns the corner
as the dogs begin turning into the alleyway.
If he were only one century old tonight
perhaps this would be amusing. The weight
of fresh blood within him slows him
and he window-shops on the long walk home.
No one seems to notice the blood all over him,
or if they do they pretend not to notice
another young man's Gothic fancy.

Now home, he waits for dawn.
The sun seems his most reluctant prey:
it just will not arrive on schedule, the clock
seems to have slowed its ticking, the intervals
between seconds get longer and longer.
When will it end? Does anyone in London
even have a rooster as harbinger
of the upcoming solar disk? The bats,
the owls, have all retired: is that red line
beyond the oak trees the edge of sunrise?

He turns to face the mirrors. It starts.
His eyes begin at last to see eyes, a face,
dark lips, those fine and perfect teeth,
the line of neck to shoulder, the skin,
as white and soft as ever he was twenty.
He leans to the glass: oh, oh,
so beautiful, so —

by some dark instinct unknown to him
his mouth finds his wrist and pierces it.
He watches himself drink from himself,
the blood flows out and inward,
an Ouroboros circle, feeder
and feeding, self-murdering Narcissus,
frozen, visible in the yellow glory
of the morning sunbeams.

He could do this forever. The sun
is doing nothing so long as he keeps
circling the fresh blood inward, outward.
If he can do to this till sunset
he will survive this burning.
Three hundred years more, at least,
he needs to exhaust his beauty.
He could take hundreds more,
or thousands; he could let
all life on earth flow through him.
It need never end.
The universe wants him in it.
Maybe he is one of the Horsemen
of universal doom and never knew it.

Sunset is only hours away.
He sways in the ecstasy of his feeding,
the sublime dream of untold victims before him.
Now that he knows the difference
between hunger and desire,
there are lists to make.
He will start with the three vampirellas.
Later, the Goth club bouncer.
Night will be his blood carnival.

THE EYE, THE MIND, THE TENTACLE

1
It always begins with an eye,
primordial   lidless
at the center of everything,
seeing all and nothing —

the skid of electrons
   from orbit to orbit,
the tug of gases
gathering into star clouds,
the whole span
of the burning spectrum
from the heart-thump pulse
   of its own being
to the X-ray symphonies
   of black hole sharks.

For time beyond time
only the eye saw,
aloof at the center
of crawling Chaos,
piping its flutes
in shrill and random harmonies —
sight without sense or reason:
Azathoth!

2

Or does it begin with consciousness?
The moment a silicon slurry
in a viscous pool of hydrofluoric
acid forms a crystalline mantle
and spins a cortex of electrons
that suddenly erupts:

I am

Or when some feeble carbon form
shambles out of the ambiote sea
and has an inkling
of its sliver of being
to roar its own defiant:

I am

Unlike the eye,
it is mortal —
its molecules prone
to ionize and slip away,
its outer shell hungry
to absorb and process matter
to keep its ego fires ablaze.

It wants to be alone
in the cosmos,
spanning time and worlds,
growing until it encompasses
all by digesting all —

it is blind, but it feeds
on the consciousness of others:
Nyarlathotep!

3
Or does it begin
with a tentacle?
A blind and nearless brainless
    worm
comes to be and crawls
toward the warmth,
its razor teeth ready.

Beneath the sea
the tentacle is king,
from the stinging lace of jellyfish
to the empire of *Architeuthis*,
the giant squid
who prowl through the inky depths
in untold numbers

larger each year
and more numerous.

The more tentacles, the more
potential power to wield and win
dominion over the others,

not a chaos of wriggling arms
but a gigapoidal symphony,
a fugue beyond fuguing,
an eros of almost infinite
   gradations.

It sleeps because it wants to.
Its patient mind is solving
a theorem
whose solution will undo galaxies
and meld all consciousness
into one self-centered being
with but one eye,
one mind,
all things obedient to itself:

dread narcissist *Cthulhu*
in ruined R'lyeh,
may you never awaken!

4
The Eye sees all but knows nothing.
The Mind sees nothing, but feeds
   on other minds.
The Tentacle imagines it sees,
   makes love to itself,
   smites matter
     with its multitude of limbs,
   and calls its hungry devastation
     genius.

This poem spoke itself
   from a dark and nameless place,
inviting unthinkable sorcery:
    to join in self the eye of Azathoth,
   the cosmic awareness
     of Nyarlathotep,
   the daring of Cthulhu.

Titans in Tartarus, in guarded sleep —
a place so deep
an anvil could fall nine days from Hell
to reach its beginning —
not even they would dare this thing.

Do not say it, do not think it,
do not make these gods
aware of you.

—April 3 2004
For the 11th H.P. Lovecraft Memorial Program
Swan Point Cemetery, Providence RI

HEARING THE WENDIGO

There is a place
   where the winds meet howling
cold nights in frozen forest
     snapping the tree trunks
     in haste for their reunion.
Gone is the summer they brooded in,
   gone the autumn of their awakening.
Now at last they slide off glaciers,
   sail the spreading ice floes,
   hitch a ride with winter.
Great bears retreat and slumber,
   owls flee
      and whippoorwills shudder.
Whole herds of caribou
   stampede on the tundra
   in the madness of hunger,
   the terror of thunder-winds..
The snow-piled Huron packs tight
   the animal skins around his doorway,
hopes his small fire and its thin smoke
escape the notice of boreal eyes.
He will not look out at the night sky,
   for fear of what might look back.
Only brave Orion witnesses
   as icy vectors collide in air.
Trees break like tent poles,
   earth sunders to craters
   beneath the giant foot-stamps.
Birds rise to whirlwind updraft
   and come down bones and feathers.

I have not seen the Wendigo —
   (I scarcely dare to name it!) —
   the wind's collective consciousness,
   id proud and hammer-hard.
To see is to be plucked
   into the very eye of madness.

Yet time and again as I walked here,
    alone in the snow
    by this solitary and abandoned lake,
I have felt its upward urge
    like hands beneath my shoulders,
    lifting and beckoning.

It says, *You dream of flying?*
    Then fly with me!
I answer *No*,
not with your hungry eye above me,
not with those teeth like roaring chain saws,
not with those pile-driving footsteps —

Like the wise Huron sachem,
    the long-gone Erie, the Mingo,
    the Seneca, the Onondaga,
like all Hodenosaunee-born,
    I too avert my eyes
    against the thing that summons me.

Screaming, the airborne smiter
    rips off the tops of conifers,
crushes a row of power-line towers,
peppers the hillside with saurian tracks,

then leaps straight up at the Dog Star,

as though its anger could crack the cosmos,
as though the sky bowl were not infinite,
and wind alone could touch the stars
    and eat them.

SQUANTO'S WIND

A ruffian wind
content till now to move
through barricades of steel
to tug of sea,
forgetful of forest and creek,
rears up at last,
howls *No* emphatically

at the Hancock tower,
a block as gray as greed,
lunging from bedrock to sky.

The primal *No* acquires more force,
plucks glass like seeds
from a ruptured grape.

The window panes explode —
a million shards
of architectural sneeze
scattered by gravity
to punctuate the streets
with gleaming arrowheads,
obsidian spears,
black tomahawks
of dispossession.

What Manitou is this
who shakes his fist
at the barons of finance?
Whatever happened to
"Welcome, Englishmen!"
(the first words spoken
by Native to Puritan)?

The engineers move in,
revise their blueprints
while covered walkways
protect pedestrians
from Hancock's continued
defenestration.

Months pass, and yet
a lingering wind remains,
circling the sheltered walks,
lapping at plywood sheets,
a sourceless gale
that ruffles Bostonians

with its reiterated cry,
not on this land you don't.

On really windy days
the whole tower sways
and workers turn green
from motion sickness.
Millions are spent
on a countersliding bed
of lubricated lead
to gyro the floor to apparent
stillness; millions more
from the slap-suited builders
on fifteen hundred tons
of diagonal braces,
all to stop
the whole ziggurat
from an inevitable topple, should
just one wind, at just one angle
bring everything down
in a snarl of pretzeled girders.
Finally all ten thousand panes
are one by one, removed
and one by one replaced.

Is Squanto satisfied
that the tower was sold,
that the new owners slid
to bankruptcy (at least
on paper), though bankers slide
from one debacle to another
and earn baronial bonuses?

No! His feathered face frowns
on clouded-over golf days.
His never-tiring gusts divert
the errant baseball, ensuring
decades of home-game dejection.

It will take more than
double-dug foundations,
wind-tunnel-tested
new window panes,
to still these vectors of rage.

Token pow-wows at shopping malls
and suburban parks
do not fool old Squanto:
sharp-dealing and inhospitable,
Boston must pay!

HERE AT THE POINT

*Secret transcript of a meeting of The Security
Committee of Swan Point Cemetery*

Here at the Point
we tolerate no nonsense.
Let the word go out
to the security guards:

photographing the monuments
is not permitted,
especially at Lovecraft's grave.

Families spend thousands
to put these obelisks and stones,
statues and mausoleums
onto our grounds

to be seen here.
Here! not in some smelly
newspaper!

If artists show up
with paints and easels,
they can depict the foliage,
but not the monuments,
not the monuments!

Use your judgment, men.
If one of those Art Club Ladies
sets up to paint, just shoo
her off politely.

But if it's a RISD[1] kid —
one of those green-haired,
snot-nosed spray painters
from the Design School,
a little ride over
to the *trespasser's shed*
might be in order.

TV crews
are absolutely prohibited —
escort them right back
to the outer gates.

As always, no picnicking!
No food or drink
whatsoever — last month
we had a whole family
eating at a graveside
(damn Armenians!).
We stopped that in a hurry.

You can't let up,
not for a moment.
Watch for those kids,
keep an eye peeled
for lurkers, and *couples*.

Matthewson here keeps a graph
of how many conundrums
we find, and where —
conundrums, you know,
those little rubber things —
disgusting!

This is a place of repose.
Repose. Why don't they get it?
No eating, no drinking,
no urinating, no fornicating,
no congregating.

---

[1] RISD. Rhode Island School of Design.

Those Lovecraft fans
are the worst. Reading their poetry,
mouthing what rituals
we can only imagine —
what the hell is *Cthulhu fhthagn*, anyway?

That Rutherford person
and those evil twins
dressed up as Lovecraft
or monks or ravens —
they have to be stopped!
Why doesn't someone stop them?

And look at their clothes,
a mockery of the good clergy
with all that black — one man
was carrying a skull! Boys with black
fingernails, Jesus! Some of the women
may not even be women.
Just imagine what they do afterward!

This Halloween, we'll stop them.
We know they're dying
to get in here at night.
Gamwell, here,
will man the portable generator.
The flood lights are set up.
The Lovecraft plot
will be as bright as day.
Just let them try to come here naked,
bringing some animal, no doubt,
to sacrifice. Not on my watch!

You, Roby, you'll get
the use of the night goggles.
Anything bigger than a badger
moves, and you'll see it.
Blair and Potter, third shift
for the two of you,
and no sleeping! I want
to see those headlights everywhere.

Next year I'll ask the trustees
to approve a guard tower
with moveable searchlights,
but I doubt they'll find the money.
What else can we do?
The ghouls are everywhere.
We just want peace and quiet.
This is a proper cemetery
and my motto has always been
As below, so above.

THE COLLECTORS

after Magritte

I know it *was* our father's house,
but prudence says he wouldn't mind
your packing up his legacies, a trunk
or two of city clothes, a photograph,
perhaps, of what had been a neighborhood
where now the sea laps barren beach
behind your yard. Do you enjoy the thought
that apple trees you climbed as a boy
are now the hanging place of cuttlefish?

Do you expect that whatever it is
that gobbles houses by night
and hauls the sidewalk off in chunks
will spare your little edifice?
I don't worry so much
about the lobsters, big as cows,
that made off with the Belgian clock,
the marble mantelpiece, or the horn
that I left in the attic; their taste
is too baroque to warrant another visit.

But I will prove, if I must
with photographs and measurements
that the oblong rock once half a mile
at sea will soon adorn the lawn,
then, with a nudge, the stairs;
next day it will bulge into the parlor;
and probably within a fortnight
sweep you a mile up the beach
to that stack of abandoned houses
where *it* has already assembled
what's left of the town.

It's one thing to be "lived through"
by Cosmic Counsciousness,
serving some higher purpose as though
the Universe had plans and we
were its chessmen. But this won't do,
this passive acceptance of
granite elbow-nudge,
this nibbling away at things,
reducing us to dust mite status
at the bottom of the vacuum bag!

QUAND IL PLEUT, IL PLEUT
DES FINANCIERS

*(Men in bowler hats descend from the clouds
in Magritte's painting, "Golconde")*

America, awake! Last night Connecticut
suffered a fall of financiers, precipitate
from aerial fleets unseen and traceable
to nowhere on or in the globe.
At dawn a gray cascade
of overcoats and bowler hats
commenced, each agent replete
with tie and unscuffed shoes,
each with a grim and businesslike

demeanor — a few, with executive
gray sideburns, clasped briefs
full of significant business plans
and letters of unlimited credit.

Only a few insomniacs
witnessed this *chute des etrangers*,
silent as dew and just as discreet,
without a flutter of parachute,
without a crease in the perfect lawns.
The anti-Newtonian host
walked with deliberate speed
to the waiting commuter trains
from whence they vanished
unnoticed into Wall Street,
courthouse and brokerage,
library and chapel, gone —
gone and never seen again!

Imposters! Who knows what plots
they hatched in their resemblance
to no one at all! Within days the banks
were belching loans; the wives at home
had well-dressed afternoon lovers;

dogs stood confused at whom to heel
or whom to bar from the kitchen door.

The birth rate rose astonishingly,
as featureless babies that refused to cry
swamped the suburban nurseries.

And this was just the start: the cloud
that made them was but a wisp
of a much larger storm, forging
its turgid thunder into an army
of Nobodies, incurable bores
intent on crowding out everyone
who's read a book or has an opinion.
Their secret handshakes and nods,
the curious little lapel pins
that your eyes can't focus on,
the sinister stripes on their ties
not corresponding to any known school
or regiment; the half-wink
they seem to use to greet one another,
smirking at others' exclusion:

these were the symptoms, alien
and alienating. There were more
like them with each passing month.
The "suits,"
as they called themselves, were here to stay.
As for the rest of us, we
were merged and acquired,
outsourced, down-sized,
shown to the door by security,
Romneyed and pension-plundered,
rezoned, foreclosed,
eminent-domained, evicted,
bankrupted and down-debited,
rust belt trailer park shantied –

just as it was planned
in their spreadsheets,
forecast in their Powerpoint
laptop PDA wireless
global master plan.

We were only here
to serve the Nobodies
on their road to acquiring
Absolutely Everything.

NOT A HYMN TO VENUS

I. EPIGRAPH
Unfair to Luna to call mad Velikovsky a lunatic,
so let us call him merely a madman. In *Worlds
In Collision* this self-taught astronomer declared fair Venus
a cosmic interloper, whose gravity-war with Mars
and brush with Earth produced the Biblical Great Flood
and a race memory of planetary dread. Nonsense
of course, but argued with passion and the paste-pot
of history and art, psycho- and anthropo- logy:
Planets as billiard balls; humans remembering
the cataclysm as a universal shriek of "Ia!"
Under its spell, I rewrote the hymn of old Lucretius
who commenced *The Way Things Are* with Aphrodite-praise.

II.
Not to you, o shining ascendant world,
morning and evening the brightest of all
in the cold night sky, not to you, Venus,
do I bring my praise and supplication.
I know from what dark nebula you came,
an apple of discord sent hurtling on
by One resenting our sweet yellow sun.
I know that man's love is not your care
for does not loveless marriage fill the earth
with more than enough starving progeny?

Young men befooled, and maidens, may worship
and make offerings at your temple door,
while in the sad garden out back, old maids
sit in a line for whoever takes them,
the last and least bargain you offer them
before they're only fit for winding sheets.
Seen from far off, so close to horizon,
your distance blinds us to your jagged teeth
which once unskinned the rock-strewn globe and sent
men howling back into ancestral caves;
nor can we see your fiery white tresses
which once ripped through our virgin atmosphere,

your poison breath of naphtha upon us,
oceans ripped into a tidal tumult,
a watery death that spared no lovers.
Your palpitations were not welcome then,
fair Venus, and even less welcome now.
Mars kicked you sunward; Earth lay in ruins
from just one passing toss of your girdle.

Meanwhile, we humans have outgrown panic.
Outward we look to the far suns, the blackness
nearly infinite between the galaxies.
We yearn to find our place of origin,
the place from which the oldest life blew down
athwart the wind between worlds, as we yearn
to endlessly invent new poems and songs,
vast fugues and operas and symphonies,
inwardly big as the outwardly vast.
We no longer backward-looking, blinded
no more by the sun we orbit, are winged.
That we yet live, upon a bleeding earth,
and dream such wide-eyed dreams, I do rejoice.
And you, Cytherean Venus — stay put!

PORTRAIT OF DORIAN GRAY

His hair is blond, gets blonder
    with each passing year.
He can discern six hundred
   shades within the spectrum.
He knows the names of all the plants
   in England. More than a hundred
works of art are sublimely,
secretly and despairingly about him.
He is more talked about at the Opera
than the reigning diva's high notes.
He has never dieted. Old clothes
from seventy years ago still fit him
perfectly. He is asked for proof of age
on entering taverns and certain clubs.
He has never gone home alone
unless it served to torment
tomorrow's conquest.

Tonight there is a detour.
He is in the old studio in Soho.
He stands before the portrait.
It is the annual visit.
The canvas looms just where
   the Master finished it,
    at just that height
that makes the viewer gasp —
the height of a dais,
   a throne
from which the portrait's eyes
can condescend to gaze —

but he is the only viewer, ever.
The skylight is painted shut,
three locks of unique form
unknown beyond the Caucasus
have never been picked or broken.

Frontispiece from First Edition of Oscar Wilde's
The Portrait of Dorian Gray, by Henry Keen.

There is only one lamp —
the one he brings,
and whose removal
returns this room
to perpetual darkness.
Its incandescence floods
the coruscated canvas
with the hard light of truth.

Older, older, older —
new lines, new sags,
new sores and venereal woes,
yellow upon yellow in eye-cast,
worms wriggling beneath

the over-stretched, parched
leather of skeletal breast
showing through tattered shroud —

He nods, and reaches up
as if to touch it, a touch
it disdains receiving.
He notes the scar
below the neck,
a thwarted lover's knife
(dead fifty years now),
around the heart
a jealous rival's bullets,
black tokens peppering
the swollen organ
(What was her name? and his?
They've both been quite forgotten!)

One gouged-out eye,
half-in, half-out
of its socket
still manages
a defiant glint
(that time he lingered
too long at the German border) —
where there were three,
not one grim tooth remains now,
the mouth shapeless, the lips
swollen in fungoid flowering.

The fingernails are black
and bent as bird-claws —
all in all
a rather appalling thing to see.

But what is this? Upon the face,
instead of its accustomed leer
of vice and lechery,
he seems to think the toothless mask
mocks him, puts on an air
of parched nobility.

"It is my place to gloat, old boy,"
the ever-young Dorian cries,
"not yours!" The good eye
of the painting just glares at him
with a kind of Mona Lisa knowing.

He backs away in nameless dread.
The eye gleams back,
its coal-black iris
encompassing
some kind of ineffable bliss,

as though it had passed beyond
the deferred death
they both would share
for all eternity.

His shaking hands switch off
the lamp; he drags it
a hundred paces to the door,
feels for the knob,
there! back and out,
latch closed, the great
amorphous locks
of adamantine steel secure.

Enough of that! He needs
the night, the London crowds!
He has his choice
of gallery openings, cafes
and garden parties.
One revel goes on all night.
A place with dark trails
and topiary monsters,
malign in moonlight,
where tipsy guests tip-
   toe to pre-arranged
couplings — one waits
beneath the favored
   weeping beech
with an embrace

he answers carelessly
with an extended kiss,
her tongue in his mouth
as lifeless as a slug.

He wrests away
and leaves her weeping
silently. He keeps
his assignation, too,
in the bamboo grove
with his latest boy
(her brother),
whom he mock-wrestles
into submission.

In after-sighs
the dull boy whispers,
"Ah, couldn't you just die
of happiness?"

Dorian feels nothing,
or feels, rather,
the dim heat a statue might,
on being worshiped.

In the darkness in Soho,
the portrait suffers a smile —
adds love to its list
of all things a man could die of.

MINERS' CEMETERY, ATACAMA, CHILE

Whatever is put in Atacama
stays in Atacama —
a wreath of roses,
every petal intact
in perfect desiccation;
miners' pine markers
untouched by rot or termite,
the wooden chapel's planks
    striated fossils,
unrusted nails a century old,
copper and tin communion cups
    all but untarnished,
the last wine's dregs
a crystal ring.

The graves are shallow,
the fence a mere
    formality,

for no one comes here —
the miners' mummies
will be miners' mummies
till the sun grows cold.

One thousand miles
of desert coast
surround this graveyard,
the vast Pacific
begrudging one drop
of rainfall,

the only damp
at the cliff-edge
and off-shore islands,
the unceasing splatter
   of guano,
     gulls' gift,

millennial deposits
a hundred yards thick,
the Andes' answer
   to Dover,

mined by coolies
for explosive nitrates,
then, as luck would have it,
the miners of Bolivia,
Peru and Chile followed
to dig the hard ground
of the desert flats
for the mountains' run-off —
more nitrates, the Titans' ichor,
without which guns
would be mere toys —
nitrates to fertilize
the sugar-beet fields
of pastry-mad Europe —

miners worked dead
in a place
where even their sweat
    was stolen.

Rain comes, on average,
just once in forty years.
If you blink,
    you miss it.
To the dead
    it has the faintest sound,
like the turning of one page.

NIGHT SHIFT

At two in the morning
three men pry the door off
of a well-kept mausoleum.
Their pickup truck,
concealed in moon-shadow
idles. I smell, from my hiding place,
    the acrid exhaust,
yew scent invaded by tailpipe vapors.
    They grunt
as a crowbar twists
the iron of a rusted lock.
One man advances
into the dead space,
stands with head bowed
as though in prayer,
    or hesitation.

The moon's full beams
illumine the chamber,
the urn, the wall plaques,
    a wreath
of shriveled camellias.
He waves the others in.
They shake their heads,
    don't want to do
whatever it is they are doing.
He puts his hands
    on their shoulders,
reminds them
of whatever it was
they promised.

He draws them in.
Together, they push aside
a stone sarcophagus lid.
They make a sickened groan,
spit epithets
in a language I do not
recognize.

They lift, drag something heavy
along the floor,
lift into pickup,
cover with tarp.

One man bends over,
heaves gobbets of puke
at the road's edge.
The other just laughs,
moves to the yew shrubs
to relieve himself.
He trembles, though,
    as he sprays the leaves.
Inches away, I hold my breath.
He staggers back, oblivious.

The truck pulls forward,
headlights doused.
The three men,
packed tight in the truck cab,
share a whisky bottle,
light one another's cigarettes,
wipe their hands on their
red plaid hunting jackets.
They watch for a long time,
wait for an interval
when no headlight is visible
anywhere, then race
for the gate and the streets beyond.

The door is left open,
   the crypt a shambles:
the open hole, wood fragments,
what might be someone's blood,
the broken lock.
I read the woman's name,
   Hungarian, I think,
   and her chronology —
   oh, a ripe one! —
   ten years dead,
ten years to the day.

THE SECRET TREE

I am dry. A circle of bark
peels stiffly from my crumbling limbs.
The itch of mold and termites
gives me no rest from entropy.
Leaves have not come this year.
It is rough everywhere:
parched earth has matted straw for hair
and desperate creatures huddle, homeless.
What the hot wind implies, I follow:
push out my roots to where the rains have gone,
deep, deeper, search for new rhythms
in crack and crevice, beyond the worm-world.

Dead to the wind above, bare-boned and tall,
I weave no banner poems in air, no seeds
fly out that other green may imitate:
making another like me is not the answer.
Mine is a secret growth, a sunless tree,
a new thing never seen before.
I plummet toward earth's mantle,
sprout from the roofs of caves,
make roost for the lightless chatterers,
the bats, my only friends in this sightless
and nearly soundless chasm.

Through the bottom and beyond, I grow.
Above, my seeming corpse, that monument,
betrays no life to deadly air. The dead things
around me are truly dead. I sway
in secret winds of magma, magnetic,
I drink salt waters from the hearts of geodes.
I bloom in the dark heart of everything,
that place, not Hades, but equally dreaded,
to which everything wants to, but cannot
fall. I have more branches now
than I ever could have imagined.

Squid sing to me in the ocean trenches,
plates moan tectonic as I wrap new rings
of iron and nickel around myself.
If leaf and blossom come to me now,
who shall see them? No one.
If seeds, or something like them,
issue from my branch-ends, where
will they go? Volcano-vented upward?
Or hoarded here in darkness?
The tree above seems only a dream now,
but so long as no one cuts it
and no storm dares to topple it,
I am only its bad dream. Pray
I do not awaken.

SINCE THE OLD ONES
CAME BACK TO EARTH

for H.P. Lovecraft's Birthday, August 20, 2009

Since the Old Ones came back to Earth,
many awaken bruised with a dim sense
of having sleepwalked, some even
appalled to find themselves
eye to eye in a canopied bed
with an equally astonished stranger;
some find themselves in half
their bedclothes, their blood-caked
fingers twined 'round the shreds
of someone's exotic lingerie, a child's
underwear, or a tuft of animal hair.
The morning mirror exam sends some
in a quick cab to the emergency room
at the sudden onslaught of hives
bearing an uncanny resemblance
to the sucker marks of an octopus,
or a face full of spiderbites,
or the distinct feel beneath the skin
as burrowing leaf-litter bugs
take up residence, eat and lay eggs;
or the incessant sneezing of one
who has passed the night in a graveyard,
acquiring minute nasal centipedes.
Doctors have diagnosed a "cosmic malaise";
Blue Cross and United have declared it
an existential pre-existing condition,
exempting only Congress and the military.

Since the Old Ones came back to Earth,
last year's brown leaves are not replaced
with new ones, and breadloaf *fuligo*,
world's largest slime-mold, ripens
putrescently 'round tree roots.

No one has ever seen
    so many mushrooms
in so many shapes and hues.
Wheat sprouts to rust, the rye to must,
young fruit to the fringe of mildew;
the produce counter is a filamented web
of blue mold, white mold, black *aspergilis*.
Old folks idling on benches, or babies
left unattended by gossiping nannies
are found enwebbed by barn spiders
the size of house cats. At sea it's worse,
as fishing boats hang in weed-clog,
cruise liners picked clean of edible beings
by hunting pods of ammoniac squid.
The warming globe proves Darwin right,
as new and ambulating gilled Things
begin to move among us,
and want brides; as yogurt mutates
into an aggressive arboreal blob
whose pseudopods seek out
and throttle the city's songbirds.

Hundreds swear they have been carried aloft
by faceless things that hugged and humped them
as strong talons held them immobilized;
crazed Carmelite nuns go belly-huge,
they claim, from angelic fetal implants.
Here in the city's wolf-hour orgies,
sleepwalkers mingle with wide-awake molesters,
who in their turn are seized
    by invisible tentacles.
Everyone has been a sex toy for something,
from every conceivable angle.
Awake, each looks at all with alarm
and embarrassment. When pregnancies
arise — and they are frequent now —
no woman knows who the father is,
or even if it's human. Just being gay
seems trivial against the thought
of twenty-organ sex, spread out
across all neurons, pulsing the span
from infrared to gamma rays.

Life, since the Old Ones came back to Earth,
means every sense and orifice
is violated: passive and paranoid
we dread the nightfall, the drowsy pillow.
Our telescopes have penetrated the universe;
now we in turn are raped by space.

AN EXPECTATION OF PRESENCES

To die is far different from what anyone supposed . . . and luckier.
—Walt Whitman

This gravesite, phantomless, does not appease
my walk — not for myself alone
have I come, but in an expectation
of presences drawn forth like tides
from that alluring moon, to sit
and hear the chattering of ghosts.
For the dead must have many songs to sing:
their dire complaints, their unrequited loves,
their broken oaths, their bony fists
clenched in the earth for some unsweet revenge;
their pleas that some neglected deed be done
to free them from a wormy pilgrimage;
their wry requests to know what souls
once famed to them, now call such pits
a hearth. But here's no tombly talk;
none but a nightbird and a tapping branch
reply to my arcane soliloquy.

My eyes, as keen
for darkness as those of an owl,
spy nothing; my ears, sensed
almost to the ultrasonic
hear nothing but bird-stir
and the limestone lap of lakebed.

Where are the ghosts?
These peaceful dead, this tranquil town
sleep far too well reposed.
          Doubts do not stalk
these penny plots, no killers wring
remorseful hands, not one protesting atheist
is doomed to somnambulist stumbling.

    Can it be
that in their simple times
(the whole of the 1800s buried here!)
mere faith
could be a perfect opiate,
that life within a wall of hymns
led to this silent, dreamless death?

Ah, so they die, who *believe* in Death,
they never rise, who sell their souls
into a cleric's dull paradise;
they never fly, who think their wings
are promises, to be attached
in worlds not one can wake to see.
O fraud of frauds, and no recourse:
no lawyer can sue an evangelist.

Yet in my heart of hearts I wish
for ghosts. For here is the depth
of all possible woe —
to leave *nothing* behind.
Nothing to strain against stars
from the haunted tips of trees;
nothing to drift like summer heat
and catch a gable's underside;
nothing to gust from cellar doors
or brood with the trunks in the attic;
nothing to serve as a core for leaves
as they fly in autumn deviltry;
no remnant left to walk the town,
no shadow over the bed, no chill
or mystery for the nervous ones —
those living yet
    who think they see the dead —
to be lost from the hands of conjurers,
not even a gleam, a shard
of phosphorescent ooze?

Oh, no, if the choice be
God's heaven or earth-bound ghost,
I'll keep my anchorage to moonlit nights,
take deed to swamps and vacant lots,
turn houses to renounced estates
abandoned to fright's hostelry;
sunbathe on monuments,
dance wild in summer thunderstorms.

Then, I shall wait for the night
when a dreaming poet comes
to my scarcely-legible tombstone,
mad as myself, my laughing heir.
What things I shall whisper
into his modern, doubting, skeptical
ear, as I reach out ...
        and take his hand.

BAI HU, THE WHITE TIGER

I dreamt — it was no dream! —
for there, on the floor, the melted snow,
the window-lattice broken, night coals
from the brazier scattered everywhere.
I dreamt he was there beside me:

the great white cat, tiger of Siberia,
lord of Manchurian wastelands. He,
my servant comes trembling to tell me,
has taken up residence
at the far end of the north pavilion.

Ah! let him stay! Bring me my sword?
No! my pen and scroll! I must wash
my thoughts with a draught of tea.
Renew the fire. Refill the *yi xing*
pot with pale white tea leaves.

"He is Death," my servant tells me.
I shake my head and answer:
"He is Autumn, the world's Fall,
my autumn, the end of my youth.
Where he treads, frost follows,

his breath the snow that fells the wheat
and makes the maples scream
red murder. Long have I known
he would be our guest one day."

"Repair the window," old Chen admonishes.
"We shall light torches to keep him off."
I see two feline eyes
grow larger in the passageway.
"It is too late. A guest once past the threshold
must be offered food and lodging.
The tiger may come and go as he pleases."

I point to where the great beast enters.
My servant issues a piercing cry.
Ignoring us, the monster, white
in the whiter moonlight, lies down
on the warm tiles of the coal hearth.
"You see, old Chen, how he reclines.
I do not think he means to harm me."
Chen bows and backs to the doorway,
and as he closes the double door, calls back,
"Tomorrow brings terror to the countryside.
The tiger will kill the fallow deer,
and, should you venture forth by daylight,
he, pretending not to know you,
will turn on you as well. An old poet
is sweet fruit after a venison banquet."

'Twixt Venus and Jupiter, one moon
hangs crescent; 'twixt sleep and dawn
the great beast cradles me, and I, him;
sword, fang, and claw forgotten, defying
our double death; a frozen interval,
two hearts abeat, and four lungs breathing.
I dream of being a great beast, rampant;
the tiger dreams of the calligraphy brush,
the tail-flick ink flow that places songs
on paper, words in the ears
of unborn readers and listeners.

I taste the blood in his mouth, the flex
of great legs that can overleap all prey;
he tastes pale tea and delicate sauces,
the savor of rare wine in a heated bowl.

As dawn breaks through,
the Heaven-tree, the willow boughs,
the distant pines sigh, shiver, shrug:
they will fight for a green day,
bird-harboring, leaf-tipped
to the lambent sunbeams.
Somewhere, out there, the tiger
drags Fall behind him as he hunts
life down with a panther frenzy.
Great clouds of birds assemble and flee
before him; cave, den, and warren
pull in their denizens for the long sleep
of winter. He leaves a trail

of antlered skeletons, doe-widows,
trees clawed clean of summer.

My place is here with lamp and teapot.
I wrote a poem. I rolled and sealed
the rice-paper scroll, wiped clean
the brush and closed the ink-jar.
This is not just any autumn's beast.
There is some cause for which
he spared me, and was not *my* Autumn
or the death-breath of *my* winter.
No, he is the Tiger of Entropy:
he drags tornados, kill-winds
and glaciers behind him.
He would blink out
the world's great cities if he could;
he would strike down the moon
as his ball-of-string plaything,
leave earth an orphan
in a sunless cosmos.
If I let him.

Tomorrow, while *he* sleeps,
wherever he sleeps —
and I see the place,
in the shade of the pines
beyond the placid river —
I shall send Old Chen for my finest mount,
my armor and my banner men.
I shall ride forth,
my flag the three-no poem of summer
defiance: *No* to death,
No to surrender, *No* to the idea
that all things must have their autumn.

I have sixty-one years
as I leave the pavilion.
I have fifty-one years as I cross
the great wheat fields.
I have forty-one years
as I track the red-maple forest.
I have thirty-one years
as I ford the river,
horse-neck and saddle
just barely above the water.
I have twenty-one years
as Old Chen passes to me
the great halberd
of my ancestors.

Now, I shall kill the White Tiger

ABOUT THE POEMS

OUT HOME

A few years back, I suddenly remembered having an IMAGINARY PLAYMATE, and was struck by the abruptness with which that activity ended. As I wrote, I remembered more. After writing the first draft of the poem, I heard the stories about draft dodgers and other runaways hiding around the coke ovens, so I added this plausible explanation of who the stranger may have been.

CHILD SEX CRIMINAL recounts my disastrous career in the first and second grades in Hecla Elementary School in Southwestern Pennsylvania. I visited the boarded-up school in the Fall of 2010 and found it exactly as I remembered, looming on a hilltop. The coal mine entrance, now sealed, is directly across the road. There is no trace of the mining machinery. I do not think the sense of rebelliousness depicted here is exaggerated, and I really was an atheist at six.

It is difficult to speak about DOCTOR JONES, the locale of which is the brick house next to the coke ovens at Carpentertown, near Hecla (some of these place names were associated with mines and have pretty much vanished from the map). It took me a lifetime to write it without getting the shakes. I will never know how much of it is true, but to the small child inside me, it is all true. You be the judge.

TORRANCE merges the very real horror of a 3,000-patient Pennsylvania mental hospital into which the state dumped psychotic killers to mingle with the general population of patients. When I discovered, on-line, a set of photographs of the ruins of this psychological snake-pit, I connected it to the "Doctor Jones" legend. When I was a child, a trip to Torrance was understood to be a one-way ticket.

NIGHTS AT THE STRAND celebrates my happy return, to the movie theater where I saw all those monster movies that so warped my consciousness. It had been boarded up in the 1970s, and then purchased and restored lovingly as the Geyer Performing Arts Center. The poem intersperses recollections of the films I saw in Scottdale starting in the third grade, with actual memories of life in the town. The visit was a profound one for me, restoring a landscape that had been ripped from me.

MONDAY MISS SCHRECKENGOST READS US *LITTLE BLACK SAMBO* brings together, in a compressed way, my experiences with race and racism up to my college years. In a deep sense, my experience as a third-grader taught me that words matter, words hurt, and that hypocrisy stinks in the eye of the universe. Even heathen kids like me figure that out. (I did attend a Bible School for exactly two weeks, and was asked to leave for posing too many embarrassing questions.) I was prompted to write this poem after the profound experience of meeting poet Marilyn Nelson, and hearing her read in

Providence. Our life is full of silences, and we need to be shaken up once in a while to break through them.

I inserted OUT HOME, a prose piece that resists poetic telling, as a sketch of a place I cannot forget, and the grandmother who was the only adult in my family I could talk to. It is truth-telling, and unveils, although ambivalently, "the things that happen to women."

My great-grandmother, the former moonshine seller, died when I was ten or eleven. I have memories of visiting her, and hearing about her Alsatian forebears. She was tricked into signing away her timber rights, which I recount in THE PINES. I changed the story a little. She was dead some years when they came to cut the trees, and it was my grandmother (her daughter) who came home one day and found the trees cut down. I took the fiction writer's privilege of combining characters and skipping generations.

BROWN DERBY is a memory of a street, on the "wrong side of the tracks," outside Scottdale.

SINKHOLES was provoked by a colloquium talk given by Prof. Jean Walton at University of Rhode Island, in which the topography of her native Vancouver was described. I think certain people need to be made to worry that the earth might open up and swallow them. The poem combines both Scottdale's old coal mines and Edinboro's mysterious little swamp.

ALL I KNOW ABOUT MY FATHER is a poem I refrained from publishing for many years. Although I corresponded with my father during his last two decades, we only met one other time in my adult life, when I was twenty. We seemed to be two people who shared only the same last name. The poem ENGLISH BREAKFASTS, although in general a satire about English reticence, also alludes to things I learned from corresponding with my father.

THE BLUE BOY. In 2010, I visited Scottdale, Pennsylvania, which I had not seen since my thirteenth year. This poem, and AT THE FUNERAL HOME, are pretty much all my memories of my paternal grandmother, Olive Trader Rutherford.

MR. PENNEY'S BOOKS is a haunting memory of my mentor in West Newton, the blighted town of my high school years. He was a retired college teacher with a vast library. When I wrote the first draft of the poem and read it to friends, one asked me why Mr. Penney had not provided for the disposition of his library, and I replied, "I don't know." Then, when I went to retype the poem in my computer, a repressed memory leaped back at me. In writing the poem, I intended only to frame it so that the final beam of light sweeping across the empty room would be the climax of the poem. It turned out that the wrenching part is in the middle, and the empty room is the denouement.

LOVE SPELLS

Poems of doomed romance come easily to me; specifically erotic poems do not. For many years I wrote elusively, toyed with pronouns, and prided myself on writing about genderless desire. Some of these poems, especially the ones set in antiquity, were always explicitly gay, but I didn't make a big deal about publishing them. When I did, it was easy enough to surround them with other poems involving Greek gods and monsters. I do not feel that I hid myself from anyone smart enough to read me carefully, but neither did I write overtly as a "gay poet." I am poet who happens to be gay. I guess I should accept at this point in life that no poem I have ever written, will ever appear in an anthology of boy-girl love poems.

Yet here, in "Love Spells," is a set of poems that does not hold back. My most obsessive puppy-love doomed passions are here in all their gloom. Two elegies for loved ones who died of HIV-related illnesses are here, too. I intersperse this grouping with the unlikely celebration of continued frisky adventures long after I should have retired with dignity from the field.

THE OBSESSION is one of my oldest poems, all the way back to Edinboro and my early New York years. A YEAR AND A DAY, IRISES, my Gothic poem FÊTE (not in this volume), and several others, are all connected via one "onlie begetter." WHAT SHE WAS LIKE came to me as an intense dream shortly after his death.

HYLLUS AND THE CHARIOTEER and BURNT OFFERING are about real people I have known, but I wrote in the voice of ancient Greek poet Anakreon, known for his sharp wit and agonized, doomed affections. HEPHAISTION AND ALEXANDER is about Alexander the Great and his lover.

TRIPTYCH is a poem I have rewritten many times over many years. It is an attempt to come to grips with the varieties of love between men. With each rewriting it has become more specific, with shards and slices of the erotic and platonic and brotherly objects of my affections.

In THE LOFT ON FOURTEENTH STREET, I adopted a long, 14-syllable line in an effort to draw out a long breath for a more Whitmanesque effect, and with the enhanced line I vowed that the poem would also be completely honest, with nothing held back. I need not explain since the poem is frankly autobiographical. The many allusions to Chinese music, poetry and culture are unavoidable since it was this friend who brought me into the world of the Middle Kingdom. I try as much as I can to make it explicate itself.

STEVEN, TWENTY YEARS AFTER was my first effort in the 14-syllable line, and its intent is similar. This shorter poem broke my barrier of silence about who and what I lost from my New York years.

PAST THE MILLENNIUM

SOLZHENITSYN IN NEW YORK was provoked by an account of the great exile attending a Bolshoi Opera performance in New York.

THE LINDEN TREE IN PRAGUE, originally titled "In Prague, A Tree of Many Colors," was my reaction to the Soviet-led invasion of Czechoslovakia in 1969. The student Jan Palach became an icon of rebellion by setting himself afire to protest the invasion of his country. The original version was somewhat obscure, and left me dissatisfied. By 1996, I finally thought the poem was finished and included it in my collection, *Twilight of the Dictators*. By 2011, details suppressed for many years by the Communist regime in Czechoslovakia were available, and I was able to extend the narrative into the events of 1989. It came to me in an instant that the undefined tree of the old poem should be a linden tree, so I added details characteristic of that tree (a familiar one from the streets of Providence). After identifying the tree I discovered that the linden tree is the emblem of the Czech Republic. After all these years, I think the poem tells the whole story, and the tree-as-narrator has been clarified. A good writing lesson from this is that a poet also needs to be a journalist.

THE BLACK HUNTSMAN is an adaptation of Victor Hugo's classic poem, "Le Chasseur Noir." I could not resist incorporating then-President Bush and the war criminal Dick Cheney among the victims of the Huntsman. So many Hugo treasures await discovery and translation.

Pieter Vanderbeck's gloomy poem "Farewell to Earth" was his final entry in *Twilight of the Dictators*, our collaborative volume about Russia and Eastern Europe and post 9/11 politics. I was compelled to answer it in my best neo-Transcendentalist, Whitman mode. My final poem in this section, THE PROPHET BIRD is both an answer to Pieter's gloominess, and a celebration of the prospects for 2009, and the hoped-for end of Cheney-Bush alarms. It was written as a New Year's valediction for my poet friends in New Jersey as well.

ARTS POETICA

WITH POE ON MORTON STREET PIER has been revised a few times over the years. Walking in Poe' footsteps is not easy, but sitting on the very pier where Poe first disembarked into Manhattan does provide a timeless Poe's-eye-view of New York. But this is a younger version of me, hell bent on my own New York adventure and just as penniless as Poe at times.

Reading Titus Livy's wonderful descriptions of Rome's founding in *Ab Urbe Condita* prompted me to imagine the great Roman law-giver, Numa Pompilius, and his Muse, the goddess Egeria. "Egeria" was also the early pen-name of Providence's poet, Sarah Helen Whitman, during the years of her marriage to a young lawyer and man-of-letters. So I can also imagine going back in time and reading this poem in Mrs. Whitman's parlor on Benefit Street.

I wrote DANNY AND BEATRICE in Prof. Peter Covino's graduate seminar on poetry, as a gentle satire on our reading of Dante's *La Vita Nuova*. Replacing the Trinity with *pi* and the rings of Hell with pasta was great fun. The place names are all from Providence's Federal Hill neighborhood, our "Little Italy."

Later, I would hear a serious colloquium talk by Prof. Travis Williams on his work on early modern mathematics printed texts, and that yielded my ARABESQUES ON EARLY MODERN MATHEMATICS.

When I attended a pre-auction show for Chinese art at Christies' in 2010, I was more impressed by a small, hand-painted fan than by almost anything else in that show. My poem attempts to show how this miniature compresses within itself the entire Chinese dream of the good life: that is, the good life available to a wealthy gentleman in the Ming Dynasty.

My poetry is littered with allusions to astronomy, nuclear physics, chemistry and biology — almost as frequent for me as calling upon some obscure Greek god. I have hesitated to footnote any of these, preferring to let them be little delights of discovery for those who get it. A poem like THE PERIODIC TABLE: HYDROGEN would take a chemistry and nuclear physics essay to untangle so I just offer it and say, as Miss Jean Brodie did, "Well, for those who like that sort of thing, there's that sort of thing for them to like." The poem URANIUM BOY in "Love Spells" is similarly rewarding for those who know how an atomic bomb is made.

VARIATIONS ON EVE. A reading by Prof. Mary Cappello from her brilliant memoir, *Called Back*, prompted me to engage in a Cappello-style "down the rabbit hole" exploration. I extended her contemplations on the word "eve" by noting that the word is itself a palindrome. The last lines of the poem are all anagrams. Being around Mary Cappello is like standing next to a Tesla coil.

ICE STORM is almost automatic writing. On the day of that storm, I sat in Kingston, Rhode Island, waiting to be called to defend my Master's project. Instead of fretting over what I was going to say, I wrote this. It makes little allusions to the topics of my portfolio, which will make better sense after I have published my research.

LUCY, A VERSE MYSTERY, continues my engagement with the sad love story of Edgar Allan Poe and Sarah Helen Whitman. It is an imaginative filling out of what little is known about Mrs, Whitman's mad sister, and it also makes an interesting connection between "The Raven" and a verse from Sir Walter Scott's *The Bride of Lammermoor.*

SOMETHING THERE IS IN THE ATTIC was a fragment from the 1970s that I had withheld. Sometime in 2011, it landed in front me and almost rewrote itself.

During my Fall 2010 trip back to Scottdale, I also visited Edinboro, to see friends and do a poetry reading. THE VANISHED CHAPEL is my reaction to seeing that my college student dwelling no longer existed. I had written an earlier poem, "Seeds from My Garden," after two return visits to the Episcopal student center where I was the most unlikely attic dweller.

HUMORESQUES

A NIGHT IN EDDIE'S APARTMENT is from Summer 2004, and recounts surrealistic impressions of a stay in Paterson, New Jersey. I thank Eddie Rivera for his hospitality, and for his permission to publish this intimate glimpse into his home life. Note: all stuffed animals in this poem were over the age of eighteen. Poet John Trause said to me, after reading the poem: "I've invited you to stay at my house. I withdraw my invitation."

Friends can point to THE ADVENTURES OF SOCK-PUPPET PETER as evidence of my mental decay: a return to adolescence, along with my sudden interest in Latin music and comic books, aka graphic novels. I am hoping that someday this bizarre poem will have its own illustrated edition. On another level, this poem is also my response to re-reading a lot of Freud during my graduate work. I hope to do some sequels with the further adventures of Sock-Puppet Peter. (He has already been to Salzburg where he appeared in a puppet version of a Mozart opera, and he was briefly held captive in the Imelda Marcos shoe collection in the Philippines.)

Presently I live in Providence, Rhode Island, in a ramshackle apartment above the warehouse of an Army/Navy store. I am sure I will to see this dwelling torn down, too. THE NEW TENANT speculates on what goes on amid all those relics of wars past.

A shorter version of AUTUMN ON MARS was written several years back and counted as part of the ongoing *Anniversarius* series. I made it longer and elaborated on the anatomy of the imaginary Martians, with a wave of the tentacle to Ray Bradbury (whose Martians were admittedly far more humanoid). But no one can say "Mars" and "Halloween" in the same breath without evoking the Master of *The Martian Chronicles*.

TWO VERSE PLAYS

CARLOTA, EMPRESS OF MEXICO is a blank verse play, based on the actual life of Empress Carlota, consort of Mexico's doomed Habsburg Emperor Maximilian. She lived on for 40 years after the Mexican disaster, confined to an asylum in Belgium. In this play, Carlota tells her story. It was a great pleasure to see this play brought to life by actresses Wendy Feller and Barbara McElroy under the auspices of the Rhode Island Writers' Circle, directed by Rose Pearson. It has had several other outings locally.

The play was written first as a monologue, with no stage directions. The opportunity to stage the play prompted me to make it a formal script, and to elaborate on the mute servant's role.

THE PRISONER is a very old poem that I recast as a two-character play in blank verse. It wound up in my master's portfolio. The events in the play are true, the characters and speeches imagined. The play has not yet been performed, alas.

SYMPHONIE FANTASTIQUE

SYMPHONIE FANTASTIQUE is derived from the first poem I ever wrote (described in my poem, "Son of Dracula"). The two surviving sections, revised and rewritten in 2011, could be read as program notes for the first and third movements of the 1827 Hector Berlioz symphony of the same title. I think it's intriguing that I began my poetry career as a response to one of the most Romantic of all Romantic symphonies, a work that sounds weird even today. And, my goodness, the Beloved is *female*. (I was fifteen years old when I write it, in a hospital bed, after a near-death experience, and surrounded by pretty nurses, so I can be excused.)

KEZIAH MASON and KEZIAH'S GEOMETRY LESSONS are imagined biographies of the witch from H.P. Lovecraft's "Dreams in the Witch House," and of Brown Jenkin, her familiar. Brown Jenkin, with his rat's body and a human face, is one of the most unsettling creatures in all of Lovecraft's tales. These are my own extrapolations, with no basis in Lovecraft's story.

AUTUMN ON PLUTO was a passing inspiration, a vision of a tree with razor-sharp obsidian leaves. The remainder of the poem flowed from that opening image. Cornelian cheery trees are planted around the Brown University campus, and I enjoy picking and eating "the food of the dead" from their branches.

DAWN elaborates on the problems vampires have with mirrors, and the ironies of the Goth obsession with costume. My vampire can see neither himself nor the clothes he dons. The ennui of the 300-year-old vampire is conveyed with a touch of Dorian Gray. I had never thought previously about pushing someone through a chain-link fence, and it does seem a novelty.

THE EYE, THE MIND, THE TENTACLE is another "occasional" poem, but it far transcends the assignment of creating something "Lovecraftian" for a gravesite reading. This one is pretty much for HPL specialists, since it includes three monstrous beings invented by The Old Gent, but I encourage others to read it — it's actually a serious philosophical poem. I take some liberties with the attributes of the mythical beings, but this is how the poem wrote itself.

HEARING THE WENDIGO is a revision of an older poem about the wind elemental known to all the Native Americans from the Deep South all the way up to the Hudson Bay. The Wendigo was first written of, and given that name, by British supernatural writer Algernon Blackwood. He learned of it during a trip to Canada. In the United States, Wendigo stories are the stuff of campfire frights, ever embellished.

SQUANTO'S WIND. The John Hancock Building in Boston had to be surrounded with covered sidewalks for several years because window panes kept popping from their casements, hurtling to the pavement below. I imagined this as the doings of an enraged *Manitou*. My early version of the poem described only the window problem. It turns out the entire construction was jinxed, so now I have added more details. Once again, more facts make is possible to have a richer and better poem. Final note: the building is also the headquarters of Bain Capital.

HERE AT THE POINT is for inquiring minds. The people who run Swan Point Cemetery, a fine and noble establishment, have some strange foibles, one of which is their mounting obsession about preventing photography of the splendid monuments and landscape of their garden cemetery. Since this conflicts with our annual Lovecraft ceremonies in Swan Point — very public events indeed — I sent a secret agent to attend the security meeting that preceded the bizarre installation of floodlights at Lovecraft's grave one recent Halloween.

The surrealist paintings of Renee Magritte are the taking-off-point for the two poems, THE COLLECTORS and QUAND IL PLEUT, IL PLEUT DES FINANCIERS ("When it rains, it rains financiers"). The first poem alludes to several paintings that depict proper row houses lined up on a seascape, another with a group of these houses piled up on a beach like a child's building blocks, and another depicting household objects in a receding line along a seashore. The second poem takes its cue from several Magritte paintings that show a huge number of bowler-hatted men either suspended in the air, or descending from the clouds. My friend Barbara A. Holland filled an entire book with poems based on the visual oddities in the Belgian Surrealist's canvases. These are my offerings in the same vein.

THE PORTRAIT OF DORIAN GRAY appeared in a shortened version in the first edition of this book, and then I suppressed it. I had not managed to express what I wanted to say, and finally I think I have arrived at my own twist on the theme of the immortal beauty and the price he pays for his immutable state. And in case you're wondering, no, it's not about anyone I know.

MINERS' CEMETERY and NIGHT SHIFT are part of my ongoing cycle, "Things Seen in Graveyards." The latter poem was a nocturnal exhumation I witnessed in the town cemetery at West Newton, Pennsylvania. On my 2010 visit back there, I determined that what I took to be a mausoleum may have been an adjacent receiving vault. Nonetheless, what I witnessed was a midnight removal.

SINCE THE OLD ONES CAME BACK TO EARTH is what might be termed a "tentacle sex" poem. Lovecraft never went beyond suggestion of what it is the creatures from other dimensions might want with us. The idea that soft flesh is a sufficient inducement for Elder God invasion is unsettling, but here it is. This was written for one of the Lovecraft birthday commemorations at Swan Point Cemetery.

AN EXPECTATION OF PRESENCES is a poem about ghosts, or their absence. Its locale is the beautiful glacial kettle lake at Edinboro, Pennsylvania, where one may stand even today in the pioneer graveyard and look out over the waters.

BAI HU, THE WHITE TIGER, has been rewritten three times in two years. I had no inkling of its defiant ending in the earlier versions. The White Tiger, in Chinese painting, is a symbol of autumn. The scholar in his pavilion may be "Meng Ch'iu Lei," a mysterious Ming Dynasty gentleman bearing my Chinese poetry name, which translates as "Dream of Autumn Thunder."

This volume is part of a trilogy containing my mature poetic work in a more-or-less chronological order: *Poems From Providence*; *The Gods As They Are, On Their Planets*; and *An Expectation of Presences* contain all the poems and revisions I consider part of my oeuvre. Other collections of my work are thematic. Sometimes the production of thematic books such as *Anniversarius* or *Whippoorwill Road* result in further revisions. In new editions of the chronological books, I attempt to keep them in synch, but it is a daunting task. Currently, I am preparing a new, revised edition of an earlier chapbook, *The Pumpkined Heart*, which will bring together all my poems related to my childhood and adolescent years in Pennsylvania. Doubtless some new poems and revisions will find their way there.

— BRETT RUTHERFORD
Providence, Rhode Island
June 23, 2012

ABOUT THE POET

Brett Rutherford, born in Scottdale, Pennsylvania, began writing poetry seriously during a stay in San Francisco. During his college years at Edinboro State University in Pennsylvania, he published an underground newspaper and printed his first hand-made poetry chapbook. He moved to New York City, where he founded The Poet's Press in 1971. For more than 20 years, he worked as an editor, journalist, printer, and consultant to publishers and nonprofit organizations.

After a literary pilgrimage to Providence, Rhode Island, on the track of H.P. Lovecraft and Edgar Allan Poe, he moved there with his press. *Poems From Providence* was the fruit of his first three years in the city (1985-1988), published in 1991. Since then, he has written a study of Edgar Allan Poe and Providence poet Sarah Helen Whitman (briefly Poe's fiancee), a biographical play about Lovecraft, and his second novel, *The Lost Children* (Zebra Books, 1988). His poetry, in volumes both thematic and chronological, can be found in *Poems From Providence* (1991, 2011), *Things Seen in Graveyards* (2007), *Twilight of the Dictators* (1992, 2009), *The Gods As They Are, On their Planets* (2005, 2012), *Whippoorwill Road: The Supernatural Poems* (1998, 2005, 2012), and *An Expectation of Presences* (2012).

Returning to school for a master's degree in English, Rutherford completed this project in 2007, and now works for University of Rhode Island in distance learning, and teaches for the Women's Studies Department. There, he has created courses on "The Diva," "Women in Science Fiction," and "Radical American Women."

He has prepared annotated editions of Matthew Gregory Lewis's *Tales of Wonder*, the poetry of Charles Hamilton Sorley, A.T. Fitzroy's antiwar novel *Despised and Rejected*, and the first volume of the collected writings of Emilie Glen.

His interests include classical music and opera, and Latin American music; Chinese art, history and literature; bicycling, graveyards, woods, horror films, intellectual history, and crimes against nature.

ABOUT THIS BOOK

The body text for this book is Plantin Schoolbook. Several attractive modern fonts, including Galliard and Plantin, are based on typefaces originally designed by Robert Granjon (1513-1589), a prolific type designer and founder active in Paris, in the shop of Christoph Plantin, and later in Rome at the Vatican. In 1913, Monotype issued several versions of Plantin, based on some of Granjon's designs, including the highly legible Plantin Schoolbook, designed by Frank Hinman Pierpont. Section titles are set in Solemnis, a calligraphic font designed in 1953 by Günter Gerhard Lange for the Berthold Foundry. Poem titles are set in Schneidler Black. The book is also decorated with several 18th-century Dutch borders and ornaments.

www.ingramcontent.com/pod-product-compliance
Lightning Source LLC
Chambersburg PA
CBHW031603110426
42742CB00037B/816